THE GCCMI BIBLE CLUB
CHILDREN WEEKLY Bible Lesson

LATEST EDITION

ARRANGED BY

GLORIOUS CHRISTIAN CHILDREN MINISTRY INTERNATIONAL

ACKNOWLEDGEMENTS

The completion of our GCCMI Children Bible study workbook for our lovelies would not have been possible without the participation and assistance of a lot of individuals contributing to this project. We would like to express our deep appreciation and indebtedness to our wonderful Bible Club Tutors; Temidayo, Sylvia, Bracy, Ruth, Joy, Mercy, Moturayo, Fisayo, Olu, Seyi, and Emmanuela for their contributions and endless support, kindness, and understanding during the project.

For these amazing children bible lessons note, to our Amazon of ideas Aunt Joy - the designer and initiator of this book, all our wonderful and supportive parents, all our glorious children, our extremely blessed sponsors, and our teachers, we say thank you.

Above all, we would like to thank the Great Almighty for always having His blessing on us.

Table of Contents

Thanksgiving	1
The Books of the Bible	3
How to Pray	6
Obey your parents	8
Self Control	10
Joshua	13
Story of Creation	17
Trust in the Lord	19
The Ten Commandments	21
The Lord is my Shepherd	23
Samuel and Eli	26
I can do all things	28
Jesus feeds 4000 men with 2 fishes and 5 Loaves of bread	30
There is time for everything	32
For God so loved us	34
Sin and its Punishments	36
Self worth/Esteem	39
Psalm 121	41
The Story of David and Goliath	43
The Parable of the Good Samaritan	45
Do not Lie	47
Psalm 91	49
The Temptation of Jesus	51
The Story of John the Baptist	53
The Beatitudes	55
Be Obedient	57

Table of Contents

The story of Daniel	59
The story of the Tower of Babel	63
Do not fear	66
Deborah	68
The story of how God chooses young David to be King	71
Do not steal	74
Jonah and the Whale	76
Be anxious for nothing	78
Forgiveness	80
You are the Salt of the Earth	82
Our Lord's prayer	84
What is Faith?	86
Why Jesus told parables	88
You are the Light of the World	92
How God Helps You in Tough Times	95
The story of Prodigal Son	97
Who are you?	99
Dip in the water	101
Keep good friends	104
The story Noah's Ark and the Flood	107
Good Communication	108
The Armour of God	111
Who is Jesus?	116
What is Giving?	118
The Power of Praise	120
God will never change	123
The Parable - God's Kingdom is a Treasure	125
The Parable of the unforgiving servant	129
The Parable - Lost Things Get Found	132

Children Weekly Bible Lesson

Topic: Thanksgiving

Introduction:

Thanksgiving simply means giving thanks, showing appreciation/gratitude for something to someone. We thank God for several things like; the gift of life, good health, the opportunity to see another new year, divine blessings, mercy, faithfulness, etc. Thanksgiving should be our daily lifestyle throughout this year, even Jesus gave thanks on several occasions in the Bible and we need to emulate Him.

For instance, Jesus gave thanks:
1. Before feeding the 4000 (Mark 8:6).
2. Before feeding the 5000 (John 6:11).
3. Before raising Lazarus from the dead (John 11:41).
4. Before sharing wine at the Passover meal (Luke 22:17-18).
5. Before breaking bread (Luke 22:19) and sharing wine (Mark 14:23) at the Last Supper.

Bible Reference:

1 Thessalonians 5:16-18, Psalm 136:1

Lessons learnt:

We have learnt three things from today's topic:
1) Thanksgiving is a lifestyle
2) When we give thanks, we get more

God delights in our thanksgiving

Activity:

Now, we are going to stand up and sing praises to God for the brand-new year 2022.

What I have learnt:

By giving thanks to God it shows that we are appreciate the things he did by thanking God he will continue to give us more

Prayer

Dear Lord Jesus, please give us grace to show You love and appreciation every day of our lives this year 2022, in Jesus' name. Amen.

Assignment:

Praise God for 10mins every day this week

The GCCMI Bible Club

GOD IS GOOD AND HIS MERCY ENDURES FOREVER

Hello there, can you draw the pictures of three things you are thanking God for?

Topic: The Books of the Bible

Introduction:

Before we learn the Books of the Bible, it is important we understand what the Bible is?
The word 'Bible' comes from the Greek and Latin word for book or books. There are 66 individual books put together in the bible - 39 books in the Old Testament and 27 books in the New Testament. The Old and New Testaments are God's written Word.

The Old Testament consists of books written before Jesus was born. It is organised into sections and each has a unique writing style in support of God's plan for the redemption of mankind (through Jesus). It consists of five sections: The books of Moses, historical books, wisdom and poetry books, major prophets, and minor prophets. While the New Testament was written after Jesus was born. It is divided into three sections: historical books, Paul's letters and additional letters.

What I have learnt:

The word bible came from the word book or books the bible has 66 books in it.

Bible Reference:

2 Timothy 2:16-17

Lessons learnt:

1. All Christians must learn and know the books of the Bible.
2. We need to read our Bible daily.
3. The Bible helps us know more about God and His principles.
4. The Bible is our earthly guide.
5. It is God's instruction for us to learn our Bibles (Joshua 1 verse 8).

Activity:

Sing the song of the books of the Bible

Prayer

Dear Lord Jesus, help us learn, know, and meditate on Your word daily, in Jesus' name. Amen.

Assignment:

Learn the books of the Old and New Testament and compose a song with them.

The GCCMI Bible Club

WORKSHEET

BOOKS OF THE OLD TESTAMENT
WORD SCRAMBLE

1. XOEUDS: _____
2. EINEGSS: _____
3. TICLEVUIS: _____
4. EAEHNIMH: _____
5. HTSREE: _____
6. CTSESEECLIAS: _____
7. ASIIASH: _____
8. SUOHJA: _____
9. ICAMH: _____
10. IODBAAH: _____
11. EPIZNHHAA: _____
12. GAGAHI: _____
13. ZEAR: _____
14. BUMRNES: _____
15. OUMENOETDRY: _____
16. HUTR: _____

Children Weekly Bible Lesson

WORKSHEET

BOOKS OF THE NEW TESTAMENT
WORD SCRAMBLE

1. NIHTIOARCNS: _____
2. IAAGNLTAS: _____
3. HIPPNLIPIAS: _____
4. BREEHWS: _____
5. STIUT: _____
6. THAMETW: _____
7. IHTTMOY: _____
8. KULE: _____
9. MESJA: _____
10. MRONAS: _____
11. EVIRTLOEAN: _____
12. OLACISNOSS: _____
13. DEJU: _____
14. SELNHASAINTOS: _____
15. PHAEISNES: _____
16. KMRA: _____

Topic: How to Pray

Introduction:

What is Prayer? It simply means talking to God. It is talking to God about something and listening to what God is telling us about that thing. As children of God, it is important we pray to God daily by expressing our gratitude, trust, confessions, and making our requests known to God. This is one of God's delights because God loves us so much. He has given us His Holy Spirit who will teach us how to pray and carry out our intercessions according to God's will for our lives. Even Jesus while on earth taught us about prayer.

What I have learnt:

_____
_____
_____
_____
_____
_____
_____
_____
_____
_____
_____

Bible Reference:

Matthew 6:9-13

Lessons learnt:

1. Pray without ceasing.
2. Our prayer is God's delight.
3. Prayer helps us to build a better relationship with God.

Activity:

Close your eyes and say a few words of prayer and try to listen and tell us what God has told you about your request.

Prayer

Dear Lord Jesus, help us to always pray to You so we can have a better relationship with You, in Jesus' name. Amen.

Assignment:

How should we pray as Christians?

Children Weekly Bible Lesson

My name is _____

The Lord's Prayer

Our Father which art in _____,

Hallowed be Thy _____.

Thy _____ come, Thy Will be done on _____ as it is in Heaven.

Give us this day our daily _____ and forgive us our debts, as we _____ our debtors.

And lead us not into _____ but deliver us from _____; For Thine is the kingdom, and the power, and the glory, forever. Amen.

Topic: Recitation Colossians 3:20 - Obey Your Parents

Introduction:

Last week, we learnt about the books of the Bible, and the importance of learning the Bible. Part of learning the Bible *is recitation which is the action of repeating something aloud from memory.*

The book of Colossians 3:20 is about obedience and God has given us little children a specific instruction to obey our parents. There are some benefits attached to this instruction if we indeed follow it. In the course of our lesson today, we shall be taught about these benefits.

Bible Reference:

Colossians 3:20

Lessons learnt:

In obedience to God and our parents in the Lord, we will have long life and prosperity.

Activity:

Compose a song or poem on obedience.

Prayer

Dear Lord Jesus, help us to always obey our parents so that it shall be well with us, and we will live long on earth, in Jesus' name. Amen.

Assignment:

Why do we need to obey our parents (answer in 3 sentences)

What I have learnt:

_____
_____
_____
_____
_____
_____
_____
_____
_____
_____

"Children, obey your parents in everything, for this pleases the Lord"

Colossians 3:20

Bible Verse Box Writing

Write the Bible verse in the boxes below

3:20

The GCCMI Bible Club

Topic: Self-Control

Bible Reference: Proverbs 25:28

Introduction:

Self-control means you can control yourself. It also means that you don't allow your emotions or desires to cause you to act in a way that you shouldn't. But sometimes it's hard to have self-control. We can't control our actions without God's help. In our Bible text, it says that a person without self-control is like a city with broken-down walls, In the Old Testament, we read about a city called, Jericho. It was surrounded by a giant wall. The wall helped to protect the people who lived inside from flood waters and those who might try to attack the city. If any part of the wall was damaged or falls down, it made the entire city open to attack to the things that the wall was protecting it from.

If we don't have self-control, then we are allowing the walls that guard our heart from sin to begin to break down. Self-control keeps us from doing whatever we want.

Lessons learnt:

1. Self-control means we think about how our actions affect others. For example: speaking with kindness towards someone you may not like, not gossiping, not complaining, using your time wisely, making healthy food choices, not hitting someone or getting in fights, etc.).
2. Self-control is learned gradually as we mature. If the Holy Spirit lives in you, He is producing His fruit in you, which includes self-control. (See Galatians 5:22-23)
3. Don't allow sin to enter your heart because the walls that protect you have been broken.
4. You can't have self-control without God, but with Him, you can do it!

Activity:

Guess Who in the Bible Game.

1. Who lacked self-control by eating a piece of fruit, even though God had commanded against it? ....
2. Who lacked self-control by giving into peer pressure and ate a piece of fruit also? ....
3. Who lacked self-control by letting jealousy control him and killing his brother Abel? ....
4. Who lacked self-control by complaining in the wilderness to Moses? ....
5. Who lacked self-control by spending all of his money on wild living? ....
6. Who showed self-control when he was tempted after 40 days of fasting? ....

Children Weekly Bible Lesson

Assignment:

1. Can you think of something you do that does not please God? ....
....

2. What is self-control? ....
....

3. Who needs to be self-controlled? ....
....

4. Why do we need to be self-controlled?
....
....

5. Give 2 examples of self-controlled behaviour?
....
....

Prayer

Dear Lord, I ask that You help me, my siblings and my parents to be self-controlled in our thoughts and actions, in Jesus name.

What I have learnt:

_ _
_ _
_ _
_ _
_ _
_ _
_ _
_ _
_ _
_ _

→ The GCCMI Bible Club

COLOR NICELY

Mandy Groce '11   ministry-to-children.com

Can you explain what you see in the picture above?

SELF-CONTROL SORT
Name _____

Read each scenario and cut them out. Then sort them.

Shows Self-Control	DOESN'T Show Self-Control

You are very excited, so you scream loudly.	Your feelings are hurt, so you write a letter.	You get angry, so you throw your book box against the wall.	You wait patiently to eat dessert until your mom says it's okay.
You are feeling angry, so you count to 30.	You yell, "I need to use the restroom" while your teacher is talking.	You are excited, so you tell your friend about it.	You are upset, so you throw a tantrum in the hallway.

Topic: Good character – Joshua

Introduction:

Joshua was a good helper to Moses. He had been with Moses ever since God led His people out of Egypt to go to the Promised Land. After Moses died, God began to speak to Joshua. Joshua encouraged the people as God had encouraged him, "Just be strong and brave." Joshua did as the Lord told him and the Israelites captured the town of Jericho. All the people heard that the Israelites had captured Jericho and they were afraid. They knew God was helping Joshua and the Israelites. They captured all the promised land. Joshua stood firm in his belief in God. He told the people, "...But as for me and my family, we will serve the Lord." Because they saw Joshua's strong faith in God, the people replied, "We would never abandon the Lord and serve other gods. So, we too will serve the Lord, for he alone is our God."

Assignment:

1. What does it mean to have a good character? List all you can think of..
   ....
2. Did Joshua possess any of the things you wrote down?...
3. When God asks us to do a task, who will supply what we need?..
4. When we accomplish something good, whom should we thank?..
5. When we don't see how a task will be done, who should we ask for help?...

What I have learnt:

_____
_____
_____

Bible Reference:

Numbers 13, Joshua 1

Lessons learnt:

1. Have faith in God – Unshakeable faith
2. Do not fear, you have God, He is Mighty and Powerful
3. Always obey – Joshua did what God wanted always
4. I can trust God to help me do what is hard
5. I can trust God to help me be strong and courageous

Activity:

Learn this by heart Joshua 1:9b Have no fear and do not be troubled; for the Lord your God is with (you) .... (Insert you name) wherever you go, BBE

Prayer

Father, help us like Joshua, to be strong in our faith and to obey what your Word commands. In Jesus' name we pray. Amen.

The GCCMI Bible Club

COLOR NICELY

Joshua Becomes Israel's New Leader

Children Weekly Bible Lesson

Joshua Explored the Promised Land Word Search

Find the words on the list that are hidden in the puzzle. The words can be left to right, up and down, or diagonally.

```
P T N I A F R A I D I J M O I
T O O N S E D E U G I O M V S
L A M Q U A T N O N S S C T R
T U E E O L O R E D E H I Q A
R R I T G R A P E S A U T V E
U A O R E R O L O R S A T E L
S U M I N C A N A A N A T V I
T I S I M N U N L A F A C I T
U N T A I I Q U A T U E R I E
L O F E L S E C T T M D I T S
N U I L K M C O N S E Q U I S
N O G S E Q U I S C I S L A N
M O S E S L E X E R I R I U R
L A O R E M O H O N E Y T E R
S U T R I B E S R E T A T V E
```

AFRAID	HONEY	MOSES
CANAAN	JOSHUA	POMEGRANATES
FIGS	ISRAELITES	TRIBES
GRAPES	MILK	TRUST

Bible Pathway Adventures

WORD SEARCH

TWELVE SPIES

```
W C K E H C G C E F E I H G R G K R K J
C H W A R I Y V X P G B V U K U U H R O
T A A M F T G T J Y H Y N U P P Y F R R
F P N K V I Q F O N X R T D B O C U W D
L G O A G E S X M A P E A S I P Z N H A
H R R M A S O R J O Q P O I P F S G I N
J W L A E N L X A V S C K L M I U P J R
M R O D P G W J F E U E W M W J E I H I
A A R O N E R B P E L E S G L V R S Q V
S Q I Y E F S A Y Y R I X J E M U D K E
Q V Y T C Z E M N S R L T C O Y F N N R
X G J C T E V H T A L L B E V S I U R B
O K N Z X W V V N U T C Y D S N H P C N
J N G G I A N T S U R E M M Q C O U M E
R U N W A N A K C G O G S S X C T T A G
R C D B W G O I A G K T Z D D U F P Y E
V B U A T R I B E S O F I S R A E L N V
D E G X H U L T K X H Y A H W E H N J I
Z W B J K I K W Z C H U Y L V F N Z C E
T Z C C A L E B A O M R J P P Y Q L F Z
```

- SPIES
- JOSHUA
- JORDAN RIVER
- JUDAH
- EPHRAIM
- ANAK
- CALEB
- POMEGRANATES
- GIANTS
- YAHWEH
- CANAAN
- ISRAELITES
- GRAPES
- CITIES
- NEGEV
- MOSES
- AARON
- TRIBES OF ISRAEL

Children Weekly Bible Lesson

Topic: The Story of Creation

Bible Reference: Genesis 1

Introduction:

We are created by God in His own image; this is how much God has loved us. In today's class, we shall learn how God created the Heavens and the Earth. We will learn more about how principled, methodological, and systematic God is, when and how God created everything we have today.

We will also learn about why we need to rest after a long day as God himself did show us an example when He rested on the 7th day of creation.

Lessons learnt:

1. God is our creator.
2. God has created everything for our benefits.
3. We need to learn how to rest.

Activity:

Draw one of the things God created and describe it (only two children will be able to show us their drawings in class).

What I have learnt:

_____
_____
_____
_____
_____
_____

Prayer

Dear Lord Jesus, You are indeed our creator, please perfect everything concerning us, in Jesus' name. Amen.

Assignment:

Mention everything God created and the days He created them.

The GCCMI Bible Club

WORKSHEET
DAYS OF CREATION

Read Genesis 1-2 with your child. Next to the correct number, write what Yahweh (God) created that day. Then color the page!

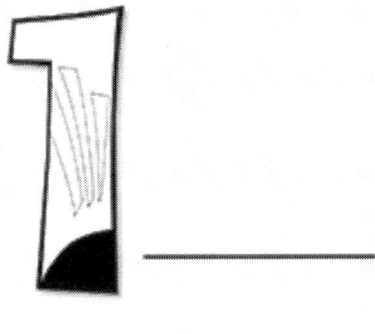 1 _____

 2 _____

 3 _____

 4 _____

 5 _____

 6 _____

 7 **Sabbath!**

Topic: Recitation - Proverbs 3:5 (Trust In the Lord)

Introduction:

It is important for us as children of God to pray to God always. God wants us to always trust in Him whenever we pray, even when the things we are praying about seem impossible. As we know with God all things are possible. So, it is important we trust in God at all times, not trusting in ourselves or our own understanding but in God who can do all things. What do we mean by trusting? It means having faith in something/someone, believing in something/someone, depending, relying, putting your hope in, etc.

Bible Reference:

Proverbs 3:5

Lessons learnt:

1. It is safer to trust in the Lord
2. With God all things are possible

Activity:

What type of things can we trust God for? Tell us

Prayer

Dear Lord Jesus, please help us to trust in you always so that we won't be disappointed in life

Assignment:

Why do we need to trust God and not ourselves (answer in 3 sentences)?

What I have learnt:

_____
_____
_____
_____
_____
_____
_____
_____

The GCCMI Bible Club

Proverbs 3:5

WORD SEARCH PUZZLE

WORDS TO FIND

TRUST	WITH	AND	YOUR
IN	ALL	LEAN	OWN
THE	THINE	NOT	UNDERSTANDING
LORD	HEART	ON	

```
V R N T V U N A C K A G
B W R R R S M Z M L V Z
E H G A N U V E L M E B
T N B U R A S Q W W N B
D H A E N E F T R P I P
A O E E I T N Q I U H W
L N O T L B O I A V T N
T M P L T T O Y H F N O
L O R D N I R E T T Q D
G D Y Z U S V A Q N W O
P N I H I V Y K E B H U
L A N W I T H X Z H H O
```

Topic: The Ten Commandments

Introduction:

What are some of the rules in your house? What are some things you are allowed to do and not allowed to do? Did you know that God has rules, too? We are going to learn about them today. God desires that we live a great life, and He has, therefore, given us some defined way of living our lives so that we live a good life that is pleasing unto the Lord.

What I have learnt:

_____
_____
_____
_____
_____
_____
_____
_____
_____
_____
_____
_____

Children Weekly Bible Lesson

Bible Reference:
Exodus 20:1-17

Lessons learnt:

God has rules and we must follow these rules accordingly

Activity:

Make sure you draw an image to describe each commandment of God.

Prayer

Dear Lord Jesus, help me to obey Your commandments and do Your will at all times, in Jesus' name. Amen.

Assignment:

Mention the 10 Commandments and tell us why God has given us these rules.

The GCCMI Bible Club

God Gave Moses His Laws
Colour by Number

Copyright © 2014 SundaySchoolZone.com. All Rights Reserved. Free to duplicate for church or home use. Visit http://SundaySchoolZone.com.

Children Weekly Bible Lesson

Topic: The Lord is my Shepherd (Psalm 23)

Introduction:

The books of Psalms in the Bible are specific praying books. Psalm 23 is the psalm of provision and protection. This is a Psalm you read when you are believing God for provision and as you read or recite it, you must trust in the Lord too because it is like praying to God. Just like David, we too can always trust in God, and we can always worship Him! Even when times seem dark or scary, or when we are happy and joyful, in every moment we should worship the LORD because He is good. Today, we shall recite our Psalm 23 and compose some songs with it.

Bible Reference:

Psalm 23

Lessons learnt:

Always read your Psalms because they are prayers too.

Activity:

Someone should compose a song with Psalm 23.

Prayer

Dear Lord Jesus, help me to read and study my Psalms and answer all my prayers as I pray with Psalm 23 this week, in Jesus' name. Amen.

Assignment:

Recite or sing with Psalm 23.

What I have learnt:

_____
_____
_____
_____
_____
_____
_____
_____
_____
_____
_____

THE LORD IS MY SHEPHERD

Help the Shepherd guide his lamb.

Children Weekly Bible Lesson

The 23rd Psalm

The Lord is my Shepherd, I shall not want. Psalm 23:1

Each number represents a letter of the alphabet. Substitute the correct letter for the numbers to reveal the coded words

1	2	3	4	5	6	7	8	9	10	11	12	13	14	15	16	17	18	19	20	21	22	23	24	25	26
Z	B	F	S	Q	Y	M	N	X	W	G	O	C	U	V	J	D	T	I	K	R	A	P	E	H	L

1. 25-12-14-4-24 _____
2. 7-24-21-13-6 _____
3. 11-12-12-17-8-24-4-4 _____
4. 4-25-24-23-25-24-21-17 _____
5. 13-12-7-3-12-21-18 _____
6. 26-12-21-17 _____
7. 23-22-4-18-14-21-24 _____
8. 3-12-21-15-24-21 _____
9. 15-22-26-26-24-6 _____
10. 10-22-18-24-21 _____

Check Your Answers

| LORD | PASTURE | VALLEY | GOODNESS | HOUSE |
| SHEPHERD | WATER | COMFORT | MERCY | FOREVER |

Topic: Samuel and Eli

Introduction:

Samuel was the son of Hannah. Hannah prayed that God would give her a son. Once Samuel was old enough, Hannah was faithful in taking Samuel to the temple to be raised there. Though Samuel was young, he learned that he must always listen to God and God gave him an important message. Eli is a prophet at Shiloh, and he was in charge of taking care, leading, and guiding Samuel in the way of the Lord. One day, God called Samuel in the middle of the night to speak to him but because he was still in training as many of you, he did not know it was God. He thought it was Eli but after several attempts, Eli taught him what to say when he hears the call again.

What I have learnt:

_____
_____
_____
_____
_____
_____
_____
_____
_____
_____

Bible Reference:

1 Samuel 3: 1 - end

Lessons learnt:

1. We must listen to the people that God has chosen to lead us in His way.
2. We must always fulfil our promise to God.
3. We must be willing to hear from God and do what He asks us to do.

Activity:

We will watch a video clip of when/how God called Samuel.

Prayer

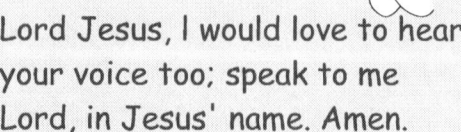

Lord Jesus, I would love to hear your voice too; speak to me Lord, in Jesus' name. Amen.

Assignment:

How many times did God call Samuel?

SAMUEL

Guide young Samuel to become a great prophet

→ The GCCMI Bible Club

Topic: Recitation Philippians 4:13 - I can do all things

Bible Reference: Philippians 4:13

Introduction:

The Bible is full of encouragement and thoughts that make it easy for us to go through everyday life. Today, we will be memorising Philippians 4:13 so that it can become a part of us and be a constant reminder of a few of the things Jesus can do for us if only we ask Him. You can say this Bible text when you feel weak, tired, or think you cannot do anything because you can do everything through Christ who strengthens you.

Lessons learnt:

1. Only Jesus Christ can give you strength.
2. It is important to rely on Jesus Christ.
3. We must always remember to ask Jesus Christ for help in everything we do daily and always.

Activity:

1. Who can share with us a time when they asked Jesus for strength?
2. Can you give us (an) example(s) of when you asked Jesus Christ for strength and what the outcome was?

What did you learn today?

_____
_____
_____
_____
_____
_____
_____
_____
_____
_____
_____

Prayer

Lord Jesus, give me the grace to always ask you for strength in everything I do. Lord Jesus, I pray that You always give me strength daily to live a godly life.

Assignment:

Send a video of yourself reciting the Bible text of our class today, then send it to your Bible Club teacher for today.

Children Weekly Bible Lesson

COLOUR THIS BEAUTIFULLY

I can do everything through Him who gives me strength

Phillipians 4:13

The GCCMI Bible Club

Topic: Jesus Feeds 4000 Men with Two Fishes and Five Loaves of Bread

Introduction:

Jesus continues to show us that He can be our provider for both our physical and spiritual needs and even more. In today's story, we can see how Jesus demonstrated His Mightiness by providing for the needs of the multitude that came to hear Him.

Bible Reference: Matthew 15:29

We can see the love and compassion in the ways and heart of Jesus by not sending them away to find food but providing for them and even exceeding the expectations of His disciples through providing more than enough for the people.

He fed these people because He is sufficient for us. He fed the people with the Word of God and also fed them with food to satisfy their physical needs. He showed that He is a miracle worker and ALL things are possible with God. He prayed and gave thanks for the two fishes and five loaves of bread before they multiplied and they had more than enough.

What did you learn today?

_____
_____
_____
_____
_____

Lessons learnt:

1. Jesus is compassionate and we also should show compassion to others.
2. We must pray for everything and on everything.
3. We should also trust that Jesus can provide for all of our needs no matter how small.

Activity:

Watch a short video clip of this story.

Prayer

Lord Jesus, help me to show compassion and love to others and everyone around me, in Jesus' name. Amen.

Assignment:

Give an example when you or someone you know showed love and or compassion to another person then send your assignment to your Bible Club.

Children Weekly Bible Lesson

COLOUR THIS

Topic: The right time (There is time for everything)

Introduction:

Lets talk about time today…. How many of you can tell time? Did you know that there are many ways to tell the time? You can use watches or clocks -- even the seasons tell us what time of year it is. What season of year is it right now? How do we know that? One way we can tell is by observing the weather around us. I think God shows himself in each season of the year and He's with us in those seasons. Ecclesiastes 3 share one of the discoveries that King Solomon made, that there are different times for different things. Not only do seasons have their purpose, but times of our lives have a purpose too. That means that there will be times when we will laugh, dance, keep, love others, be loved, and have peace. There will also be times when we will cry, mourn and grieve, give up, fix something that is broken, and have to deal with war.

Bible Reference:

Ecclesiastes 3:1-8

Lessons learnt:

1. There is time for everything
2. God is with us no matter what we feel, where we are or what we are doing

Activity:

Draw a clock.

Prayer

Dear Lord, teach me the right way to live and how to live Christ-like. Thank you, Lord, for keeping my family safe, in Jesus' name, Amen.

What did you learn today?

_____
_____
_____
_____
_____
_____
_____

Assignment:

Create your own list of time. For example: A time to play; A time to tidy up. A time to be loud; A time to be quiet and so on. and stick to them

Children Weekly Bible Lesson

Topic: Recitation John 3:16 - For God so loved us

Bible Reference: John 3:16

Introduction:

This memory verse is a must-know for any child of God because it sums up the love of God for us and the sacrifice God made to fulfil His love. God loves the world and He showed us by sending His Son to come and die for our sins and all we have to do is to believe and confess that Jesus is Lord, then eternal life is ours. This is a verse of confession, adoption into the kingdom of God, and whoever is ready to give their lives to Jesus as their Lord and Saviour.

Lessons learnt:

1. How much God loves us.
2. God sacrificed His Son for the sins of humanity.
3. If you believe in Him, your soul will be saved.

Activity:

Everyone must recite John 3:16 (as class time permits)

Prayer

Lord Jesus, I believe you are the son of God and I confess you as my Lord and Saviour.

What I have learnt:

_____
_____
_____
_____
_____
_____
_____

Assignment:

Write out John 3:16 boldly on a cardboard/paper, with coloured pen, glitters, crayons, and paint (anything and everything to beautify), take the picture of your artwork, and send it to your Bible Club teacher.

Fill in the missing letters.

For _____ so loved the _____, that he gave his one and only _____, that whoever believes in _____ should not perish, but have eternal _____

John 3:16

Topic: Sin and its punishment

Introduction:

Children, today we are going to learn about a time when two people told a lie and what happened to them afterwards. A lie is a sin. Sin is anything you do, say or think that displeases God. God takes dishonesty so seriously. Dishonesty can destroy marriages, families, churches, relationships and our witness. It hurts us, it hurts others and it hurts God. If we are honest, even when we make a mistake, things can be made better. Remember that every thing you do affects your relationship with your heavenly Father. Let's read the story.

Assignment:

Make sure you speak only the truth from today onward.
I,..will speak the truth from now hence forth so help me God. (Insert your name above)

What I have learnt:

_____
_____
_____
_____
_____
_____
_____
_____

Bible Reference:

Acts 5:1-11

Lessons learnt:

1. We can never hide from God; why hide anyway!
2. God sees everything, even what we keep in secret
3. When we lie, we lie to God and not to men
4. Greed will always cause us to commit sin
5. Never fake an image of generosity

Activity:

Have you ever told a lie? It is very serious. But God tells us we can say we are sorry and start telling the truth. Let's read what the Bible says: Do not lie to each other. You have left your old sinful life and the things you did before. Colossians 3:9 (ICB)

Prayer

Lord, when I'm tempted to lie, help me rely on your strength to tell the truth. I can do all things through Christ who strengthens me, thank You

ANANIAS & SAPPHIRA

Acts 4:32-37 – Acts 5:1-11

Across

2. When Peter confronted Ananias he said, "You have not lied to men, but to _____!"
5. In the early church, many Christians sold their land and _____ and gave the money to those in need.
7. A great _____ seized the church when they heard what had happened to Ananias and Sapphira.
9. _____ hours after Ananias, Sapphira came before Peter to offer her portion of the sale money.

Down

1. Peter said to Sapphira, "How could you conspire to test the _____ _____ and lie about the money?"
3. Which apostle did Ananias and Sapphira give their money to?
4. As soon as Peter confronted him, Ananias _____ instantly.
6. Peter asked _____ if she was offering the full amount of money she received from the sale.
8. Instead of giving all the money from their sold property away, Ananias and Sapphira decided to _____ some of it for themselves.

ANANIAS & SAPPHIRA

Spot 8 differences between the two pictures.

Topic: Self-worth/Esteem

Introduction:

Has anyone has ever found money just lying/crumpled on the ground. Where did you find it and what value of money did you find? Was it clean or dirty? Was it still worth the value that was printed on it when it was made? Our value is not determined by how others see us or even ourselves; it is based on what God says about us. We are marked "valuable" by Him. We should view every person valuable and worthy.

Lessons learnt:

1. In the beginning God created us in His Own image
2. Sin (our disobedience, our not believing & trusting what God said and Who He is) caused us to become damaged. We became crumpled and dirty just like the money you found.
3. Sin is damaging, but it does not change our worth to God; His grace continues to pursue us.

Bible Reference:

Romans 5:8

Activity:

Repeat this:
I..
(Your name) am special and worthy of God's love. God loves me and my family so much and I love Him too.

Prayer

Dear God, thank you for making me special and for making me "me." Thank you for giving me the ability to _____. (Name something you are good at.) Help me use this talent to honor You. Please help me to remember that I am special because You made me in Your image (Genesis 1:26-27). Help me to remember that I am valuable because You created me. Amen.

Assignment:

Write beautiful things about yourself. You could write I'm special. In all of creation, there's nobody like me. Nobody looks exactly like me. Nobody talks exactly like me. Nobody's handwriting is exactly like mine; nobody likes all the same things that I do, nobody has all the same skills that I do. God made only one "me," so I'm very special to Him and so much more...Get a picture of you and stick it by your write up and put it were you'll always find it.

What I have learnt:

_____

_____

_____

God Demonstrates His Love Word Search

```
N N Y M K M L X G O D V S S L
G P O W E R L E S S Q U E F X
S J G U N G O D L Y O T X R V
I U R D C H S T K E A Y F N T
N O O H L F V U T R L P K E K
N D C L R M R H T E N F M S P
E H I O S S G S R S J H C G O
R T L U D I N A K E I E Q J S
S H O W R O R X N S V P D C S
A D V F M V G O M L L D V H I
R A E E V W Y B S P A I L R B
K R D H X N M E E L K E D I L
J E T Y A B A X H C W D D S Y
X Q I U E N N G O O D Y K T G
S C W H L L H W R O Z Q Q V Z
```

Find the underlined bold print words in the puzzle.

You see, at just the right time, when we were still **powerless**, **Christ died** for the **ungodly**. Very **rarely** will **anyone** die for a **righteous man**, though for a **good** man someone might **possibly dare** to die. But **God demonstrates** his own **love** for us in this: While we were **still sinners**, Christ died for us. Romans 5:6-8 (NIV)

Topic: Psalm 121

Introduction:

Psalm 121 is one of the psalms of protection that was sung by people journeying to Jerusalem on pilgrimage, and it is one of the ascent psalms. This psalm will help you to know that you are always protected, and God is always watching over you in the house and even when outside. This psalm is sometimes sung or read.

What I have learnt:

_____
_____
_____
_____
_____
_____
_____
_____
_____
_____
_____
_____
_____

Bible Reference:

Psalm 121 (read out loud with your teacher)

Lessons learnt:

1. Trust in God's protection.
2. God helps every Christian in tough times.

Activity:

We will be watching a video of Psalm 121 and we will dance to it.

Prayer

Lord, please help me to constantly remember that you are my divine protector.

Assignment:

Read Psalm 121 then write down the verse that stands out to you the most.

COLOUR THIS BEAUTIFULLY

I pray, and the Lord comes to help me.

Topic: The story of David and Goliath

Introduction:

You may already know about the boy named David who fought and killed a giant named Goliath. Goliath was a mighty warrior who was more than nine feet tall. He was a GIANT! God helps us overcome the "giants" in our daily life. We might not face a nine-foot giant, but we face giants of other kinds like fear, loneliness, and failure. Please, let's open our Bible to read: 1 Samuel 17

Lessons learnt:

We have learnt 5 lessons from this story,
1. We must have courage. (1 Samuel 17:32) You will use courage to face giants in your life.
2. We must have confidence. You can have confidence that God will help you overcome the problems you face.
3. We must be prepared. (1 Samuel 17:40) It's important for you to prepare to face the challenges in your life, too.
4. We must put our trust in God. (1 Samuel 17:45) When you face problems, put your trust in God, not in your ability.
5. We have victory. (1 Samuel 17:47). When you turn your battles over to God, you'll have the victory over the giants in your life.

What I have learnt:

_____

_____

_____

Children Weekly Bible Lesson

Bible Reference:

1 Samuel 17

Activity:

Repeat the words courage, confidence, preparation, trust, and victory and narrate the story of David and Goliath.

Prayer

Dear God, just as You gave David the victory in his battle with Goliath, I know that when I put my trust in You, You will give me the victory over the giants I face in my daily life, in Jesus' name. Amen.

Assignment:

1. Why were King Saul and his army afraid?
2. What did Jesse ask David to do?
3. Why was David not afraid of Goliath?
4. Why did Saul think David couldn't fight Goliath?
5. How did God prepare David to fight Goliath?
6. How did David fight with Goliath a) with his fists b) with Saul's armour and weapons or c) with the Lord/s power?
7. Name something that can be an enemy in our lives?
8. How will God help us fight our enemies?

COLOUR THIS BEAUTIFULLY

David & Goliath

Topic: The Parable of the Good Samaritan

Bible Reference: Luke 10:25-37

Introduction:

Jesus is a really great teacher. He taught important lessons in a lot of different ways. One of the ways He used a lot was telling stories. Can anyone tell me what we call the stories Jesus told, which are written down in the Bible; the stories Jesus told in order to teach us important things? Today, we would look at one of the parables Jesus told. Please, let's open our Bible and read Luke 10:25-37.

Lessons learnt:

1. Love your neighbour.
2. Be generous.
3. Treat others the way you want to be treated.

Activity:

Narrate the parable of the good Samaritan.

What I have learnt:

_____
_____
_____
_____
_____
_____
_____
_____
_____

Prayer

Dear Father, Jesus taught us to love our neighbour. Help me to be a good neighbour to everyone I meet, in the name of Jesus we pray. Amen.

Assignment:

1. How should we treat others?
2. Who is my neighbour?
3. This week, make a list of people to whom you can show kindness, just like the man in The Good Samaritan parable.

The GCCMI Bible Club

COLOUR THIS BEAUTIFULLY

The Good Samaritan

Topic: Do not Lie - Proverbs 12:22

Bible Reference: Proverbs 12:22

Introduction:

Not everyone knows all ten of the Ten Commandments, but even those who only knew a few remember this one: Thou shalt not lie. When God gave the Ten Commandments, He made it clear that dishonesty was a sin. Please, let's open our bible and read Proverbs 12:22. Telling the truth takes courage, but it's always easier to tell the truth the first time than to admit you lied later. Make a resolution this week to be a truth-teller. Stop using little lies to get what you want. Be the kind of person who can always be trusted.

Lessons learnt:

1. We learnt that it's not okay to lie, not even a little lie.
2. Also, when you start telling lies, they can keep growing and growing very big (You tell another lie to cover up the first lie and another and another).
3. We learnt that God loves it when He can trust us and the best way to do that is to tell the truth always.
4. We learnt that lies destroy our character before others.

Activity:

Discuss - Is there ever a time when it's okay to lie?

Prayer

Dear God, help us to be truth-tellers. Forgive us for the times when we lied. Give us the courage to tell the truth the first time and resist the temptation to tell little white lies.

What I have learnt:

_____
_____
_____
_____
_____
_____
_____

Assignment:

Telling the truth takes courage, but it's always easier to tell the truth the first time than to admit you lied later. Make a resolution this week to be a truth-teller.

Stop using little lies to get what you want. Be the kind of person who can always be trusted.

The GCCMI Bible Club

COLOUR THIS BEAUTIFULLY

Lying lips are an abomination to the Lord: but they that deal truly are His delight.

— PROVERBS 12:22 —

Children Weekly Bible Lesson

Topic: Psalm 91

Introduction:

Have you ever watched a hen with her chicks? They are really interesting to watch. The little chicks follow their mother everywhere she goes. She leads them all over the barnyard showing them where to find food while watching over them. The little chicks know not to wander far from her. Whenever the mother hen thinks there is danger, she lifts her wings and the little chicks all come running for cover. She protects them from the wind, rain, and heat of the sun by covering them with her wings. She keeps them warm with the heat from her body. She keeps them dry like an umbrella. The Bible tells us that God is a lot like a bird or hen who protects and watches over her chicks. He watches over us and protects us, so we don't have to be afraid. Please, open your Bible and read Psalm 91.

Bible Reference:

Psalm 91

Lessons learnt:

1. God is stronger than anything else in the entire universe, so we never have to wonder if He is truly able to protect us from evil. He can and He always will.
2. The Lord is our refuge, or shelter from evil. He promises to help us and even sends His angels to guard us against harm.

Activity:

Why does He protect us?

Prayer

Father, we thank You for Your loving kindness, for taking care of us and protecting us, in Jesus' name.

Assignment:

Memorise by heart, Psalm 91: 1-16

What I have learnt:

_____
_____
_____
_____
_____
_____
_____
_____

WRITE OUT THE VERSES OF PSALM 91 BY HEART

Topic: The Temptation of Jesus

Introduction:

Have you ever been tempted to do or say something that you know is wrong? For example, you knew you had homework that needed to be done, but your favourite programme was airing on TV, so you chose to watch TV instead of doing your homework. The next day when your teacher asked you why you didn't turn in your homework, you told the teacher, 'My dog ate it' or 'My baby brother tore it up'. We begin to point the finger of blame at someone else. It isn't a sin to be tempted unless we do what we are tempted to do even though we know it is wrong. Even Jesus himself was tempted. In our Gospel lesson today, we read about the temptation of Jesus. Please, let's open our Bible and read Luke 4.

What I have learnt:

_____
_____
_____
_____
_____
_____
_____
_____

Bible Reference:

Luke 4

Lessons learnt:

1. Jesus fully trusted and followed God. He rebuked His tempter by speaking God's Word back.
2. We should always look to God's Word and ask Him to help. If we do sin, we can ask God to forgive us because Jesus died in our place for our sins.

Activity:

We all face temptations, don't we? What are examples of some of the temptations you face?

Prayer

Father, we are thankful for your Holy Word. Help us to read our Bible daily and hide its words in our hearts so that we might be able to resist temptations, in Jesus' name we pray. Amen.

Assignment:

1. How many times was Jesus tempted?
2. Mentioned the ways and what He replied to his tempter?

The GCCMI Bible Club

COLOUR THIS BEAUTIFULLY

Jesus spent 40 days in the desert, and the serpent came to tempt him. But Jesus used God's words to stand up to the serpent! Matthew 4

Can you see the Serpent?

Topic: The Story of John the Baptist

Introduction:

John the Baptist was the man chosen by God to announce the birth of Jesus and the works He would do on earth. In this story, we will learn about who the parents of John the Baptist are, how John the Baptist was born, and his major assignment on earth.

What I have learnt:

_____
_____
_____
_____
_____
_____
_____
_____
_____
_____
_____
_____
_____

Bible Reference:
Luke 1

Lessons learnt:

1. God can tell us what He wants us to do.
2. God can use anybody to do His work.
3. We should not doubt the power of God but always believe when He speaks.

Activity:

Tell us a story of how God has spoken to you.

Prayer

Dear Lord, give me the grace to always believe in you whenever you speak.

Assignment:

Narrate the story of the birth of John the Baptist

The GCCMI Bible Club

JOHN THE BAPTIST

Lead Jesus to John the Baptist

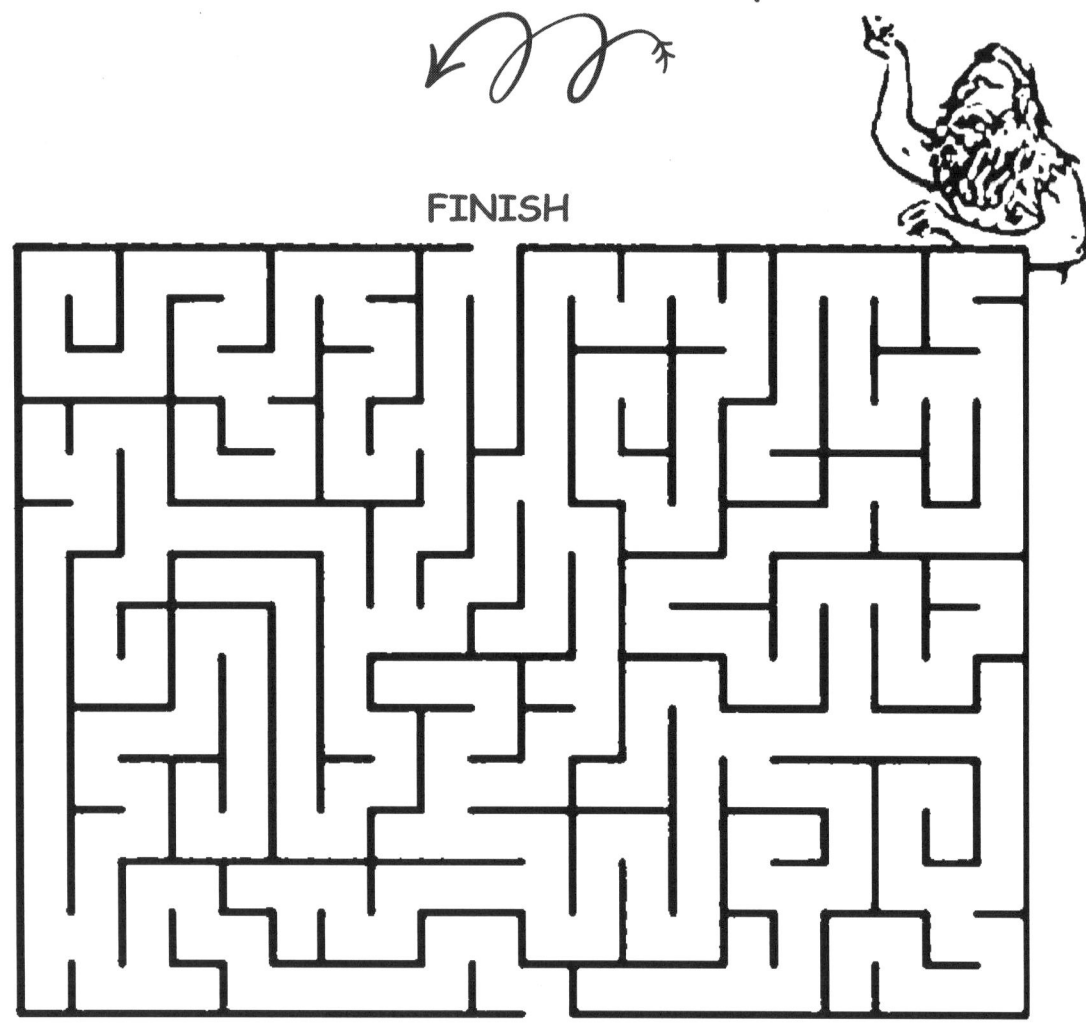

FINISH

START

Topic: The Beatitudes

Introduction:

The beatitudes are the teachings on the blessings of God spoken by Jesus to the multitudes when He was on a mountain. In this lesson, we will learn about all the beatitudes written in Matthew 5:3-12.

What I have learnt:

_____
_____
_____
_____
_____
_____
_____
_____
_____
_____
_____
_____
_____
_____

Bible Reference:

Matthew 5:1-12

Lessons learnt:

1. We are to live our lives according to what is written in the beatitudes.
2. We will receive the blessings of God if we do what the beatitudes say e.g. when we are merciful to others God will show us mercy.

Activity:

Tell us one way you have enjoyed any of the blessings from the beatitudes.

Prayer

Jesus, thank You for the blessings you have given to us, give us the grace to do Your will.

Assignment:

Recite the beatitudes.

»» → The GCCMI Bible Club

BLESSED are:
Matthew 5:3-10

1.

2.

3.

4.

5.

6.

7.

8.

Topic: Be Obedient

Introduction:

In this lesson, we would learn about what the Word of God says about obedience, those we are to obey, and things we do that show we are obedient children of God.

What I have learnt:

_____
_____
_____
_____
_____
_____
_____
_____
_____
_____
_____
_____
_____

Bible Reference:

Ephesians 6:1

Lessons learnt:

1. Obedience means to do as you are told.
2. Obedience also means to follow instructions, rules, and regulations given to us by our parents, elders, school, and even country.
3. Obedience is a commandment from God, and we must do it so we can make heaven.
4. When we are obedient, we enjoy God's blessings.

Activity:

Tell us one way you have been obedient.

Prayer

Father, help me to always be an obedient child to You, my parents, and elders.

Assignment:

Recite Ephesians 6:1

OBEDIENCE

Doing what i have been asked the first time completely, joyfully and without complaint

Topic: The Story of Daniel

Introduction:

In the Bible there is a verse that says, "Trust in the Lord with all your heart and lean not on your own understanding; in all your ways submit to him, and he will make your paths straight." That verse is Proverbs 3:5-6. It means that when we stick close to God, he will guide us to the right path for our life. Today we are going to learn about a man named Daniel. When things got tough for Daniel he decided to stay with God. God rewarded his faithfulness in a big way.

Activity:

Sing "Daniel Chose to Follow God" to the tune of "Mary Had a Little Lamb"

God tells us to follow Him, Follow Him, Follow Him
God tells us to follow Him, and He will make our path straight.
Daniel chose to follow God, Follow God, Follow God
Daniel chose to follow God, and God saved Daniel.
I can choose to follow God, Follow God, Follow God,
I can choose to follow God, and be just like Daniel.

Bible Reference:

Daniel 6

Lessons learnt:

1. The Bible teaches us that when we trust God, He keeps our path straight. Daniel decided to stick close to God and trust that God's way is the best.
2. God would rescue His faithful children
3. Godly character requires discipline
4. Always ask God for help like Daniel did in prayers

Prayer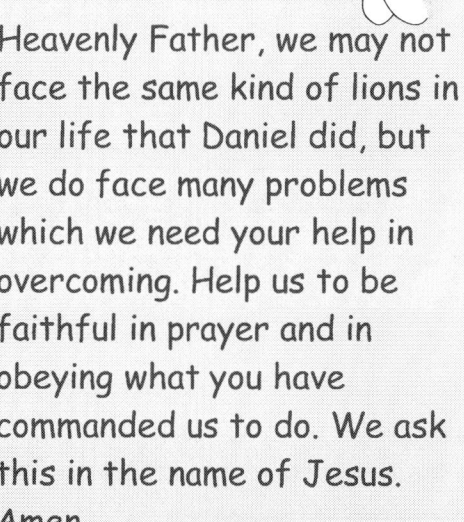

Heavenly Father, we may not face the same kind of lions in our life that Daniel did, but we do face many problems which we need your help in overcoming. Help us to be faithful in prayer and in obeying what you have commanded us to do. We ask this in the name of Jesus. Amen.

» → *The GCCMI Bible Club*

Assignment:

1. Who is Darius?..
2. Why were they looking for something that Daniel had done wrong in his life?
   ....
3. Why was Daniel safe in the lions' den?
   ....
   ....
4. What happened to Daniel's enemies?
   ....
   ....
   ....
5. What can you do this week that will be a positive influence in another person's life?
   ....
   ....
   ....
   ....

What I have learnt:

God's Prayer Warrior: Daniel

My God sent his angel to shut the lions' mouths so that they would not hurt me, for I have been found innocent in his sight. Daniel 6:22 (NLT)

The puzzle is based on Daniel 6:1-28.

```
A Q L C Y G H F A U N O Z S M
R Y L P T T P J N S X I Y X Z
R T N Q U G R E O E B Q G B X
E Y L O A C A X O R T P D H K
S Z M M Z P Y Y N V Z O A U T
T Y F E L U E B Y E J D N X R
E Y M M S B D D J T Q D I A E
D G M W O N V E Y Y L A E X S
S H U T J R U N B L G R L W C
M Q C L X N N Q Y A V I C S U
X I Q W I F A I T H F U L H E
Y H I C R O I G N D W S D M D
L T C K K H N V H G E X D O D
A N G E L T V S Y N A N B G B
D H N M P U D E E E J G U A F
```

ARRESTED	PRAYED	DARIUS	SHUT	SERVE
MORNING	ANGEL	RESCUED	MOUTH	LIONS
NOON	DEN	FAITHFUL	NIGHT	DANIEL

Children Weekly Bible Lesson

Bible Pathway Adventures

DANIEL WORKSHEET
DANIEL AND THE LIONS

Open your Bibles and read Daniel 6:19-22.
Fill in the Blanks. Color the picture.

"King Darius rose early in the _____ and hurried to the _____ den. When he came near to the den, he cried out and said to _____, "Daniel, servant of the living _____, is your God whom you serve continually, able to deliver you from the lions? Then Daniel said to the king, O _____, live forever. My God has sent His _____ and has shut the lions' _____, and they have not hurt me; because as I was found _____ before Him and also before you. I have done nothing wrong."

Topic: The Story of the Tower of Babel

Introduction:

Do you know what happened in the book of Genesis when the people of Babel thought they could build a tower to the heavens and show God and others their greatness?

After the flood, God told Noah and his family to have children and spread out around the world. But instead, the people settled in one place. Then, they began building a tower so that those who came after them would think they were great and would admire their accomplishments. Higher and higher they built, brick upon brick. God wasn't happy about their stubborn hearts. So, He confused their languages, forcing them to finally do as He'd asked, which is to spread out around the earth.

Assignment:

1. How does God see a stubborn person?
2. What are the dangers of being stubborn?
3. Read Genesis 11:1-9 and tell the story of the tower of Babel.

What I have learnt:

_____
_____
_____
_____
_____
_____
_____

Bible Reference:

Genesis 11:1-9

Lessons learnt:

1. We should not do things that will not glorify God.
2. Unity can cause any group of people to achieve what they want.
3. Bragging and boasting does not bring honor to God.
4. You are valuable because God specially formed you and loves you.
5. God sometimes intervenes in human affairs.

Activity:

Tell us a story of how you worked with a group of people and if you all achieved the goal.

Prayer

Lord Jesus, take away the spirit of pride in me. Dear God, give me the grace to only do the things that glorify You.

The GCCMI Bible Club

BIBLE QUIZ

TOWER OF BABEL

Read Genesis 11:1-9. Match the question with the answer on the right.

Questions

____ Why was it easy for people to work together to build the tower of Babel?

____ How high did they plan to build the tower?

____ Who came down to see the tower?

____ How did Yah (God) stop their work?

____ Why did the people stop building the tower?

____ What was the name of the place where they tried to build the tower?

____ What does the biblical name Babel mean?

____ What happened to the people?

____ What materials did the people use to build the tower?

____ What did the people think the tower would protect them from?

Answers

1. Land of Shinar
2. Yah (God)
3. God scattered them all over the earth
4. To the heavens
5. They all spoke one language
6. Confusion
7. Being scattered
8. Brick and bitumen
9. He mixed their languages
10. They didn't understand one another's speech

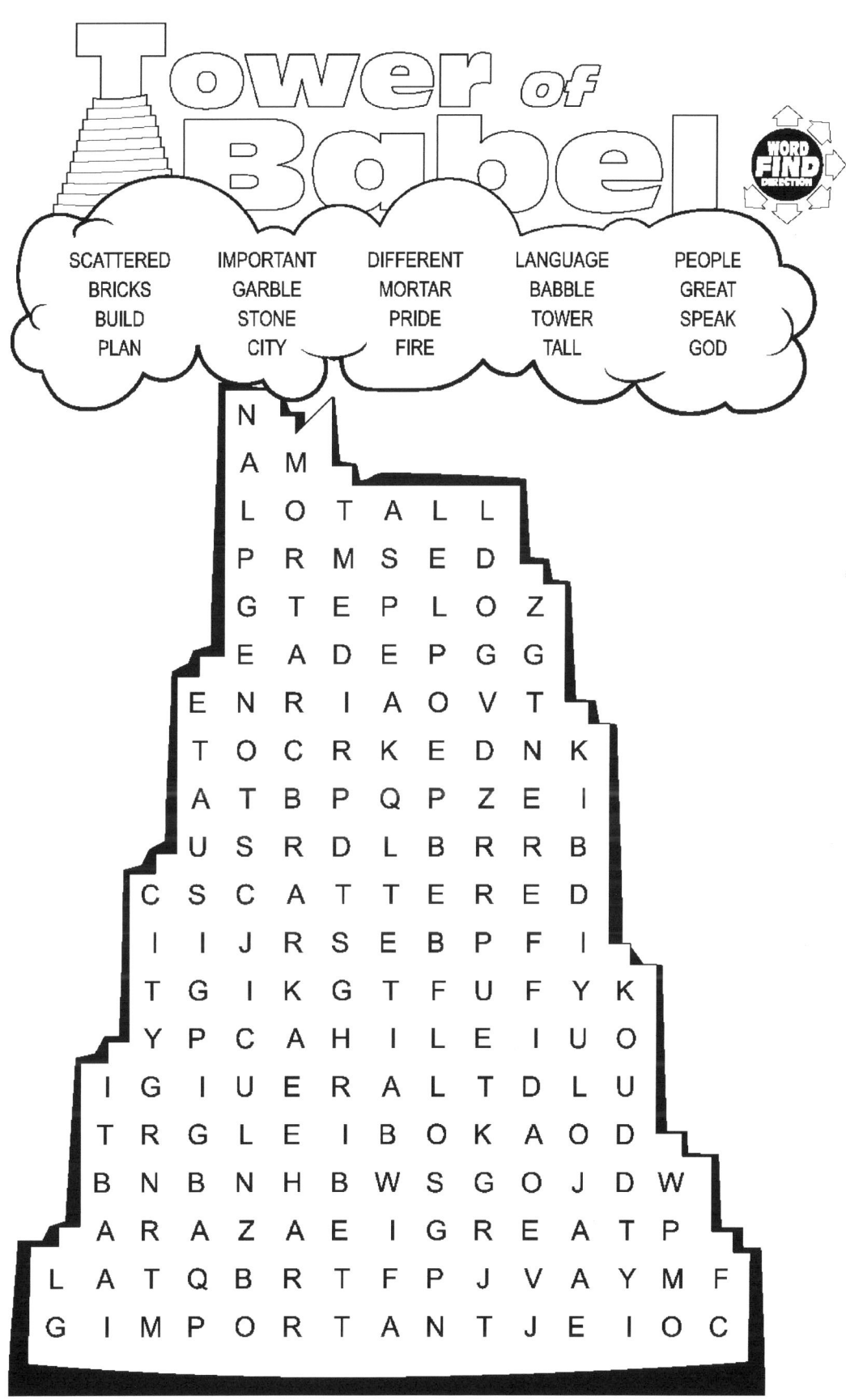

Topic: Recitation Do not fear Psalm 27

Introduction:

God does not want us to worry or have fear about anything because He has given us a sound mind. The lesson today teaches us not to be afraid of anything because we have been saved by Jesus Christ.

Activity:

This week do these 3 things in response to Psalm 27

- Write a verse from the passage you want to remember
- Write a reason to praise God that you see in the Psalm
- Draw something from the passage that you think is important

What I have learnt:

_____
_____
_____
_____
_____
_____
_____
_____
_____
_____

Bible Reference:

Psalm 27

Lessons learnt:

1. The Lord has promised to protect and keep us safe so we shouldn't be afraid of anything.
2. We should not be afraid even in times of trouble because God will hide us away from evil.
3. Be strong and brave and always wait for God to help you.

Prayer

Lord thank you for protecting me and my family always, thank You Lord in Jesus name.

Assignment:

Read and recite Psalm 23.

Colour this Beautifully
Memorise Psalm 27:1

The LORD is my Light and my SALVATION Whom shall I FEAR? The LORD is the STRONG HOLD of my LIFE... of WHOM SHALL I Be AFRAID? — Psalm 27:1

Topic: A Brave Woman - Deborah

Bible Reference: Judges 4:1-24

Introduction:

One of the Judges in the bible was a woman. Her name was Deborah. A judge was someone God would send to help his people, to save them from their enemies. Deborah is the only judge described as a prophet. A prophetess is a woman whom God chooses to convey His special messages to others. Since God told Deborah what to say, the people went to her to have their quarrels settled and so on. She was so wise that everyone wanted to listen to what she said. She used to sit under a palm tree and let people come and ask her advice. Israel's enemies were very mean. Let's read her story.

Lessons learnt:

1. God calls ordinary people even you
2. God helped Deborah lead the Israelites, His help is available to you
3. We should trust God even when no one does
4. When God goes before you, you have nothing to fear

Assignment:

1. What was the name of the woman Judge?
   ....
2. Who was the general of God's army?
   ....
3. Why did Deborah go with Barak into the battle?..
   ....
4. How did the Israelites win against an army with 900 iron chariots?........................
5. Where did Sisera, the general of the enemy's army hide? ....
6. Who killed Sisera?...............................

Activity:

Song
I'm in the Lord's Army
I may never march in the infantry
Ride in the cavalry
Shoot the artillery
I may never shoot for the enemy
But I'm in the Lord's army!

Prayer

I thank You Lord that You love to do extraordinary things through an ordinary child like me and for making me brave and always providing help for me.

What I have learnt:

_____
_____
_____

COLOR BEAUTIFULLY DEBORAH THE JUDGE

Deborah Was a Judge in Israel Word Scramble

Unscramble each of the clue words. Take the letters that appear in the circle boxes and unscramble them to find the answer to the last phrase.

MORTS

SIPERA

AANANC

KABAR

WORDS

BORHAED

What did Sisera have that scared the Israelites?

He had 900 ⬜⬜⬜⬜⬜⬜⬜⬜ .

Children Weekly Bible Lesson

Topic: The story of how God chooses young David to be King

Introduction:

Bible Reference: 1 Sam 16:1-13

Whenever God went looking for a king, everyone expected him to pick the biggest, tallest, and strongest person. Instead, He picked the smallest person. Who is the tallest here? Who is the smallest in age? If you are the youngest in your family stand up. Do you ever feel left out of some things because you are the youngest? God chose the youngest in this story. He chose a boy. Most scholars believe David was around twelve years old at this time! Also, God cares about what's inside, not how we look. Let's listen to a story about how God picked King David.

Lessons learnt:

1. God doesn't care how we look as long as we have a heart that loves him.
2. God not only chose David, but David chose God
3. God didn't wait until David grew up to call him and use him. God prepared David for his future even while he was a young boy
4. Where was David when Samuel came to Jesse's house? (Out tending the sheep) David spent time alone with God out there in the pastures. He spent time praying and worshipping and even thinking about Bible verses (Psalms). God used all that to help David become the "incredible" king who could shepherd the people of Israel. David could also play the harp. God used David's talent to help King Saul feel better.

Activity:

Share something that you can do to show love

....
....
....
....
....
....
....
....
....
....

Prayer

Dear Father, thank you because truly You have a plan and purpose for my life. Thank You, that You have chosen me and created me to be INCREDIBLE! In Jesus' precious name, Amen.

> The GCCMI Bible Club

Assignment:

1. God had Israel's next king ready to be anointed. Was Samuel eager to fetch him? ....

2. How were prophets received in Israel at that time?
   ....
   ....

3. Where was David from?
   ....

4. Was David declared king when he was anointed?
   ....

What I have learnt:

Samuel Anoints David

CSHOEN ☐☐☐☐☐☐
             2

SPERHEHD ☐☐☐☐☐☐☐☐
            1

ATONIN ☐☐☐☐☐☐
       3   5

LROD ☐☐☐☐
       4

Man looks at the outward appearance, but the LORD looks at the _____ .
    1 Samuel 16:7b (NIV)

☐☐☐☐☐
1 2 3 4 5

Bible Memory Verse

The LORD does not look at the things man looks at. Man looks at the outward appearance, but the LORD looks at the heart.
1 Samuel 16:7 (NIV)

Topic: Do Not Steal

Introduction:

To Steal means taking what does not belong to you. One of the ten commandments says, 'You shall not steal'. For God to be happy with us, we must obey His commandments which include not taking what does not belong to us (stealing).

What I have learnt:

_____
_____
_____
_____
_____
_____
_____
_____
_____
_____
_____
_____
_____

Bible Reference:

Exodus 20:15

Lessons learnt:

1. Stealing is bad and is a sin.
2. A child of God must not steal.
3. Always ask for permission before taking what's not yours.
4. You will be blessed by God when you do not steal and obey all of God's commandments.

Activity:

Tell us a story of how you overcame the temptation to steal.

Prayer

Father, thank You for always providing for me and my family. Help me never to take what does not belong to me.

Assignment:

What does it mean to steal and what does God say about stealing?

Children Weekly Bible Lesson

Colour the picture below.

What is she doing in the picture?..............................

Is this ok?...

DO NOT STEAL

Topic: Jonah and the Whale

Introduction:

The story of Jonah and the whale is the story of love and disobedience. God loves everyone including those that do not revere Him just like the people of Nineveh. So, God in His mercy, compassion, and grace sent His prophet Jonah to them but because Jonah knew how great the sin of the people of Nineveh was, He did not want them to repent and turn to God, so he ran away from God. God's faithfulness and love made Jonah end up in the belly of the whale and God made him go to Nineveh to let them know about the judgement of God.

What I have learnt:

_____
_____
_____
_____
_____
_____
_____
_____
_____
_____
_____
_____

Bible Reference:

Jonah 1

Lessons learnt:

1. God loves us.
2. He will always take us back when we ask Him for forgiveness.
3. Our forgiveness MUST be real and true.

Activity:

Watch a video clip about Jonah and the whale.

Prayer

Lord Jesus, help me to forsake my sins and rely ONLY on You, in Jesus' name. Amen.

Assignment:

Draw a picture of a whale and write the Bible text of today next to it, then paste it where you can see it every day as a reminder of God's forgiveness.

Children Weekly Bible Lesson

Colour the picture below.

Can you see Jonah?..

Is it good to disobey?..

Topic: Recitation Philippians 4:6-7 - Be anxious for nothing

Introduction:

Today's Bible text and our topic are focused on the following themes: Worry, prayer, supplication, thanksgiving, and the peace of God.

The Bible text is reminding us that we should not worry, think or get depressed about anything but to always pray and let God know what we really want, only then are we going to have peace.

What I have learnt:

_____
_____
_____
_____
_____
_____
_____
_____
_____
_____
_____
_____

Bible Reference: Philippians 4:6-7

Lessons learnt:

1. We need to pray always.
2. We need to let God know what we need/want.
3. The peace of God is our right as a child of God.

Activity:

Recite and read along with your Bible Club teacher the Bible text for today.

Prayer

Lord Jesus, help me to always rely on You and pray for what I need rather than worry about it, in Jesus' name. Amen.

Assignment:

Write out the keywords from this Bible text and find out their meanings. Then read the bible text again and send your thoughts to your Bible Club teacher.

Children Weekly Bible Lesson

Phil 4:6 Match the Icons Bible Verse Review

Philippians 4:6

"Do not be ☆_____ about 🌼_____

but in 🌀_____ situation, by ❋_____ and

☺_____, with ♡_____, present your

✿_____ to God.

❋every thanksgiving scared jealous questions god peace requests anything, justice contend your true rest joy petition along love prayer mean anxious

Topic: Forgiveness

Introduction:

There are many verses in the Bible that talk about forgiveness, but we will only take a few of them. The Bible talks a lot about forgiveness maybe because it is one of the values in our Christian faith. Forgiveness is letting go of any wrong that anyone has done to you directly or indirectly. This means that we do not keep a score or account of how many times someone wronged us. We must learn to forgive others, whether they apologise to us or not because Jesus also forgives all our trespasses, so it is important we forgive others so that God can forgive us.

Bible References:

Matthew 6:14,
Luke 23:33-34,46,
Luke 15:11-32,
Matthew 18:21-22

Lessons learnt:

1. Forgiveness is important to our Christian faith and life.
2. God wants us to forgive those that have wronged us.
3. Forgive and you too shall be forgiven.

Activity:

Share when you have forgiven someone in the past or when someone has forgiven you.

Prayer

Lord Jesus, help me to forgive others even when it is difficult for me to do, in Jesus' name. Amen.

Assignment:

What does FORGIVENESS mean?
FOR OLDER KIDS:
Research and write out 5 verses from the Bible that talk about forgiveness. Write your answers and send them to your Bible Club teacher.

What I have learnt:

_____
_____
_____
_____
_____
_____
_____
_____
_____
_____
_____

Children Weekly Bible Lesson

COLOUR THIS BEAUTIFULLY

Confess what is written on the picture

I can forgive others

Topic: You Are the Salt of the Earth

Introduction:

Salt is a preservative, and it was commonly used in ancient times to keep things fresh (this was in the age when there was no fridge or freezer to keep things). Salt used to be of great value like gold and in some cases, it served as currency. Salt can alter the chemistry in cooking and even keep roads from freezing (during winter for those in cold countries). Salt can give flavour good or bad (It can worsen the food you just want to flavour if in excess)

Today, we will talk about an illustration Jesus gave the disciples to show us how the children of God should behave and interact with others on earth. Jesus is telling us that we have to be preservers of good and great things, behaviour, attitudes, and moods wherever we go to. We must be set apart from our friends and people that do not know Jesus Christ.

We must continue to make the earth a better place with ALL and everything that we do.

What I have learnt:

_____
_____
_____
_____
_____
_____
_____

Bible References:

Matthew 5:13

Lessons learnt:

1. You are set apart for God.
2. Let your behaviour, attitude, moods, dressing, talking, and even listening reflect you as a child of God.

Activity:

Sing the song, This little light of mine, I'm going to let it shine x2 let it shine, let it shine, let it shine.

Prayer

Lord Jesus, I will love to be salt on this earth, please help me and bring people into my life to help me become salt on earth, in Jesus' name. Amen.

Assignment:

What is the difference between being salt of the earth and being sugar of the earth?

Children Weekly Bible Lesson

"You are the Salt of the Earth"

In Matthew 5:13 Jesus says we are the salt of the earth. Salt is known for being very pure. Circle the actions below that show how we can be pure and share our God-like nature with others.

Sharing

Comforting

Fighting

Acting Mean

Getting Angry

Helping

Topic: Our Lord's Prayer

Introduction:

Prayer is communicating with God as a child of God. It's very important you speak with God every day, just like you cannot do without speaking with your Daddy and Mummy. In this topic, we will be talking about how God wants us to pray, we will see what prayer should entail.

Bible References:

Matthew 6:9 – 13

Lessons learnt:

1. God is waiting for you to pray to Him, He loves to hear your voice.
2. You cannot survive as a Christian without prayer.
3. Jesus loves it when little children pray.

Activity:

Share your testimony of answered prayer with us.

Prayer

Lord Jesus, please teach and help me to pray to You always, in Jesus' name. Amen.

Assignment:

Recite Matthew 6:9-13.

What I have learnt:

_____
_____
_____
_____
_____
_____

Children Weekly Bible Lesson

The Lord's Prayer

Our Father, who art in heaven,
Hallowed by Thy Name,
Thy Kingdom come,
Thy will be done,
On earth as it is in heaven.
Give us this day our daily bread,
And forgive us our trespasses,
As we forgive those
who trespass against us.
And lead us not into temptation,
But deliver us from evil,
For Thine is the kingdom,
and the power, and he glory,
for ever and ever.
Amen.

Color carefully and frame this page for your room

Topic: What is Faith?

Introduction:

Faith means trust, believe. Faith is also complete trust in something or someone. Hebrew 11:1
In the Bible, faith is defined as the substance of things you hope for, the evidence of things not seen. Having faith means that we believe even if we cannot readily have physical proof/evidence of what we hoped for. Can we see God? Not necessarily, but we see a lot of what He has done and continues to do. The Bible talks about people who demonstrated faith. There were people like Noah, who built an ark in anticipation of a flood that had not started yet. Abraham, who left his home to follow God, or David who had faith in God that he could kill Goliath. These people showed great faith in God. Can we be like those heroes in faith too?

What I have learnt:

_____
_____
_____
_____
_____
_____
_____
_____
_____
_____

Bible References:

Hebrew 11: 1

Lessons learnt:

1. God expects you to have faith in Him.
2. You cannot receive anything from God without faith.
3. Faith in God protects our hearts from worldly things.

Activity:

Share how having faith has helped you so far.

Prayer

Heavenly Father, please increase my faith in You.

Assignment:

Mention 3 people in the Bible who showed faith in God.

Children Weekly Bible Lesson

Name:

Hebrew 11

1.) How are you putting your faith in Jesus?
_____
_____
_____

2.) What is faith?
_____
_____
_____

3.) How did Noah have faith in God?
_____
_____

4.) Without _____ it is impossible to please God. (Hebrews 11:6)

Topic: Why Jesus Told Parables

Introduction:

Who likes stories? What are some of your favorite kinds of stories to read and listen to? Why do you think we like stories so much? Stories are fun! We get to use our imaginations and learn new things through stories. We also have an easier time remembering things we learn, when we learn them through a story. Did you know that Jesus told stories, too? Why do you think he told stories? Jesus is a really great teacher. He taught important lessons in a lot of different ways. One of the ways he used a lot was through telling stories. Can anyone tell me what we call the stories Jesus told, which are written down in the Bible?

Activity:

Mention some parables that Jesus told in the bible.

_____

_____

_____

Prayer

Jesus – I know that You made me and want me to obey You with all my heart. I know I have disobeyed and wanted to be my own boss. I have thought and done things against your directions. I am sorry. I know that you gave up his life to save me from these sins and make me your child again. I accept your promises and ask you to please save me now and forever. Amen.

Bible References:

Matthew 13:10-17

Lessons learnt:

1. Jesus taught directly and sometimes He used parables
2. Only the people really interested in Jesus' teachings understood His parables
3. Those with hardened hearts didn't understand Jesus' teachings
4. To understand Jesus' teachings in the bible, ask God for wisdom
5. The parables are all different kinds of stories, dealing with different kinds of people in different situations. But they all have one thing in common. All the parables are about the Kingdom of Heaven.

Assignment:

Look through your bible and pick any parable you like and read and summarize it and send a copy to Aunt Joy

Children Weekly Bible Lesson

What I have learnt:

The GCCMI Bible Club

The GCCMI Bible Club

Topic: You Are the Light of the World

Introduction:

A lamp gives light to everyone in the house. How will you feel if there's no source of light in your room? You will not feel okay, I guess. That shows that light is very important at home or anywhere.

Without light, darkness will take over. When Jesus told us that we are the light of the world, He was telling us who we are supposed to be. We are to be children of God everywhere we find ourselves. We should act in such a way that others see Jesus in us.

John 8:12, 'Then spoke Jesus again unto them saying, I am the light of the world: he that follows me shall not walk in darkness but shall have the light of life Jesus expects us to be the light just as He is the light'.

What I have learnt:

_____
_____
_____
_____
_____
_____
_____
_____

Bible References:

Matthew 5:14

Lessons learnt:

1. You cannot be the light of the world if you do not have Jesus Christ in you.
2. Darkness cannot stay where there is light. This means that with Jesus in you, you can overcome all challenges that come your way.
3. Jesus expects you to be a good example for others anywhere you find yourself.

Activity:

Discuss what the environment will look like if there is no light.

Prayer

Dear God, make me a shining light to the world.

Assignment:

Memorise by heart Matthew 5:14

Children Weekly Bible Lesson

Colour the picture below.

You are the light of the world, always remember this

Topic: How God Helps You in Tough Times Psalm 121

Introduction:

Bible References: Psalm 121

Every child of God faces challenges. It is important to know that every person will face challenges in their lives, especially Christians. For example, you might be having some difficulties in some subjects. But the encouraging thing is that God is here to help you through your challenges. (Read Psalm 121).

Lessons learnt:

1. God helps every Christian in tough times: In verse 2 of our text, it says that our help comes from God. In other words, God should be the first person we turn to in times of challenges. When we talk to God about it, He will send help to us.
2. God watches over your life from beginning to end. We call Him Alpha and Omega. He knows the end from the beginning. Therefore, God knows who you will become, He holds your future in His hands. He wants to help you through life's most difficult times.
3. God is always with us, providing strength and shade.
4. Rejoice: Dance and be happy because you have a Father who watches over you. How wonderful it is to note that God watches over each of us!

Activity:

Memorise Psalm 121: 1

Prayer

Thank You, Lord, for assuring me that my help comes from You. Thank You, Jesus, for watching over me and preserving my life.

Assignment:

Get a plain sheet of paper and a marker, write Psalm 121 verses 3, 4, and 5 on it. Paste it on the wall in your bedroom. Read it every day before you sleep.

What I have learnt:

_____

_____

_____

The GCCMI Bible Club

Go through the maze to find out who the boy gets his help from.

"I will lift up mine eyes unto the hills, from whence cometh my help."

Topic: The Parable of the Prodigal Son

Introduction:

Jesus told a parable about a man with two sons. A parable is a simple story to help people understand something that is important. Jesus told this parable so that people would understand something about God. Sometimes, we are like the younger son in the parable. When we do things that are wrong, we start to feel very bad. We might think that God would never forgive us. But God does forgive us! When we tell God we are sorry, He is so happy. He is happy because he loves us, and He always wants us to do the right thing. Our Heavenly Father is like the father in the story. He throws a party when we repent and turn back to Him. There is rejoicing in heaven when we say we are sorry. (Luke 15:7).

What I have learnt:

_____
_____
_____
_____
_____
_____
_____
_____
_____

Children Weekly Bible Lesson

Bible References:

Luke 15:11- 32

Lessons learnt:

1. God is always happy when we return to Him.
2. There is rejoicing in heaven when we tell God we are sorry.
3. God forgives us no matter the weight of sin.

Activity:

Memorise the verse 1 John 1:9
1. Do you think God will love and forgive you if you tell Him you are sorry for something?
2. How do you tell God you are sorry?
3. How would God feel when you tell Him you are sorry?

Song:

Jesus loves me, Yes I know, For the Bible tells me so
Little ones to Him belong, They are weak but He is strong.
Yes, Jesus loves me, Yes, Jesus loves me, the Bible tells me so

Prayer

Thank You, Jesus, for loving me, thank You for showing me that You are always there to receive me when I turn back to You. Lord, I pray that You help me to love You more and listen to Your instructions. Amen.

The Prodigal Son's Journey
(Luke 15:11-32)

Follow the maze to discover the prodigal son's journey from when he left home to his return home. Label the parts of the story in each area of the maze.

Topic: Who Are You?

Introduction:

Like the other Apostles, Peter travelled to different towns and started Churches in all the towns he visited. Later, after he left those towns, he would send letters back to the churches to teach them more about God. (Read 1Peter 2:9-10). Let's take a look at who Peter says we are!

Bible References:

1 Peter 2:9

1. WE ARE A CHOSEN PEOPLE: God chose us to be His people. God who created everything, chose you! God loves you that much.

2. WE ARE A ROYAL PRIESTHOOD: what does royal mean? It means that you are a king or a queen or that you're in the king or queen's family. We are royal because we're in God's family and God is the King of the whole universe. We are Princes and Princesses in God's kingdom.

3. WE ARE PRIESTS: A priest is another name for pastors. Priests pray to God for people and tell them about God.

4. WE ARE HOLY: This means we are special and different. As God's children, we believe what God wants us to believe and do what God wants us to do. We obey God's rule and do the right things, even if other people don't.

5. WE ARE THE LIGHT: He has forgiven our sins and showed us mercy for all the wrong things we have done, Jesus took our place. So, remember how special you are. You are God's royal child. He chose you to follow Him and to teach other people about Him and He forgave us all our sins.

Lessons learnt:

1. I am a royal priesthood.
2. I am a Priest.
3. I am holy.
4. I am light.

Activity:

Memory verse: Romans 8:28
Song: We are a chosen generation by Sinach.

Prayer

Father, we thank You for sending Jesus to take our punishment for us and for making us Your special, royal children. Help us to live the way you want us to so that we can honour you, in Jesus' name we pray. Amen.

What I have learnt:

_____
_____
_____
_____
_____
_____
_____
_____

Color the Prince or Princess that you are

Prince ↑   ↑ Princess

Topic: The story of how God heals Naaman - Dip in the water

Introduction:

Bible References: 2 Kings 5:1-19

I'm sure everyone here has been sick at one point or another. What do you do when you are sick? Usually people go to a doctor, take medicine, get lots of rest, and maybe eat a bowl of chicken soup or two. Most of the time, medicine, and a day or two of rest is all we need to get well. Right? But not always. There are some sicknesses that never go away. Sometimes people get diseases that they have forever. No matter how many bowls of chicken soup they eat, their sickness doesn't go away. Our story today is about a man named Naaman. Naaman had a disease that wouldn't go away. There was no cure! His disease was called leprosy. A person infected with leprosy has bumps on their skin or what looks like a bad rash. Back in Naaman's day it was a big deal to get leprosy. It meant that no one wanted to be around you because they were afraid, they would get it too. There was no way to hide the fact that you had leprosy. As soon as a person saw you, they would know right away. Today we're going to hear how God healed Naaman's disease.

Lessons learnt:

1. Believers (children) can encourage others to turn to God when they have difficulties.
2. You and I can make a difference in the lives of the people that God puts in our lives by using every opportunity to do what pleases Him. Show others how there truly is a God who so loves the world!
3. One way to show love to others is by telling them about things that will help – God want us to help others
4. Make yourself available to God like the little girl in our story

Prayer

Help me to be like that little servant girl and be ready and willing to tell others that Jesus died for their sin, that He rose again, is seated on the right hand of the Father, and is coming again in glory to judge the living and the dead. Thank You that whosoever believes on Him will not perish but have everlasting life. AMEN.

→ The GCCMI Bible Club

Assignment:

1. Who is Naaman?
   ....
2. What difficulty was Naaman facing?..............................
3. How did the slave girl from Israel use the opportunity God had given her?
   ....
4. When Naaman went to Elisha what did Elisha do?
   ....
   ....
5. Why was Naaman angry?
   ....
   ....
6. How did Naaman's servant use the opportunity that they had to help Naaman?
   ....
7. How was Naaman healed?..
   ....
8. Why did Elisha refuse to take Naaman's gifts?
   ....
9. How can you encourage others to believe in God's promises and obey Him?
   ....
10. Who had the power to cure Naaman?
    ....
11. What does this story teach us about God?
    ....

What I have learnt:

_____
_____
_____
_____
_____
_____

Elysha Healed an Army Captain
Spot the Differences

Compare the picture on the top with the picture on bottom. Circle the 18 things that are different.

Topic: Keep good friends

Introduction:

Today, we're talking about "FRIENDS." We have friends at school, at soccer, at dance and at other places that are either causing us to grow closer to Jesus or causing us to draw away from Jesus. The way to grow closer to Christ is by what we do; by reading our Bibles and praying, but our friends play a BIG PART too. There are things we can do every day that make our hearts grow closer to Christ. Like talking to God. What else makes us grow closer to Christ? Mention some. When we do these mentioned things, what happens to our heart? It grows!

When we hang out with bad company those who would draw us away from Jesus. They start to corrupt or mess up our good character that we've learnt from the Bible. Like talking to God every day, reading God's Book, going to God's House, treating others with kindness.

Dear children, we've got to do like Jesus tells us in His Word in James 4:8, "Draw near to God and He will draw near to you." Friends are great (either Christians or non-Christians), but please don't let them take over your life WHY? Because some of them may draw you away from Jesus.

What I have learnt:

_____
_____
_____
_____
_____

Bible References:

1 Corinthians 15:33

Lessons learnt:

1. Your heart is precious, you must guard it
2. The friends you hang out with can influence you
3. Choose your friends wisely

Activity:

Memory verse: Romans 8:28
Song: We are a chosen generation by Sinach.

Prayer

Let's bow our heads and pray about who are our friends, and if we're allowing them to take over our lives. Pray for wisdom to choose your friends wisely.

Assignment:

How does bad company corrupt good manners?

_____
_____
_____
_____
_____

FRIENDS

How are we to treat our friends?

Luke 6:31	1 Thess. 5:11	Ecc. 4:9-10

The opposite of good friends: Read 1 Corinthians 15:33

What does this verse say will happen if you have bad friends? _____

How does God say to pick your friends in Proverbs 12:26?

_____

Why? _____

What does the Bible say about

Proverbs 12:26

Proverbs 13:20

Proverbs 18:24

friendship

Proverbs 22:24-25

Luke 6:31

1 Corinthians 15:33

Children Weekly Bible Lesson

Topic: The story of Noah's Ark and the Flood

Bible References: Genesis 6:8 -22

Introduction:

Today's story is about righteousness found in a man called Noah and how he obtained the favour of God to scale through the judgement of God. It is more than just about the man Noah, but the grace he obtained. God will always look down to see everyone. He provides the route of escape and that is salvation in the form of the ark for the people. Neglecting the salvation provided has a consequential effect

Lessons learnt:

1. God is looking for a righteous man.
2. God will always judge sin (Roman 1:22)
3. He provides a route of escape for the judgement; that is salvation.

Assignment

1. What is righteousness
2. How can we escape the judgement to come?

Prayer

Let's pray that the Lord will help us to abide in Him and we would not neglect the salvation of God

What I have learnt:

_____
_____
_____
_____
_____

NOAH'S ARK
AND THE GREAT FLOOD

Spot 8 Differences between the two pictures

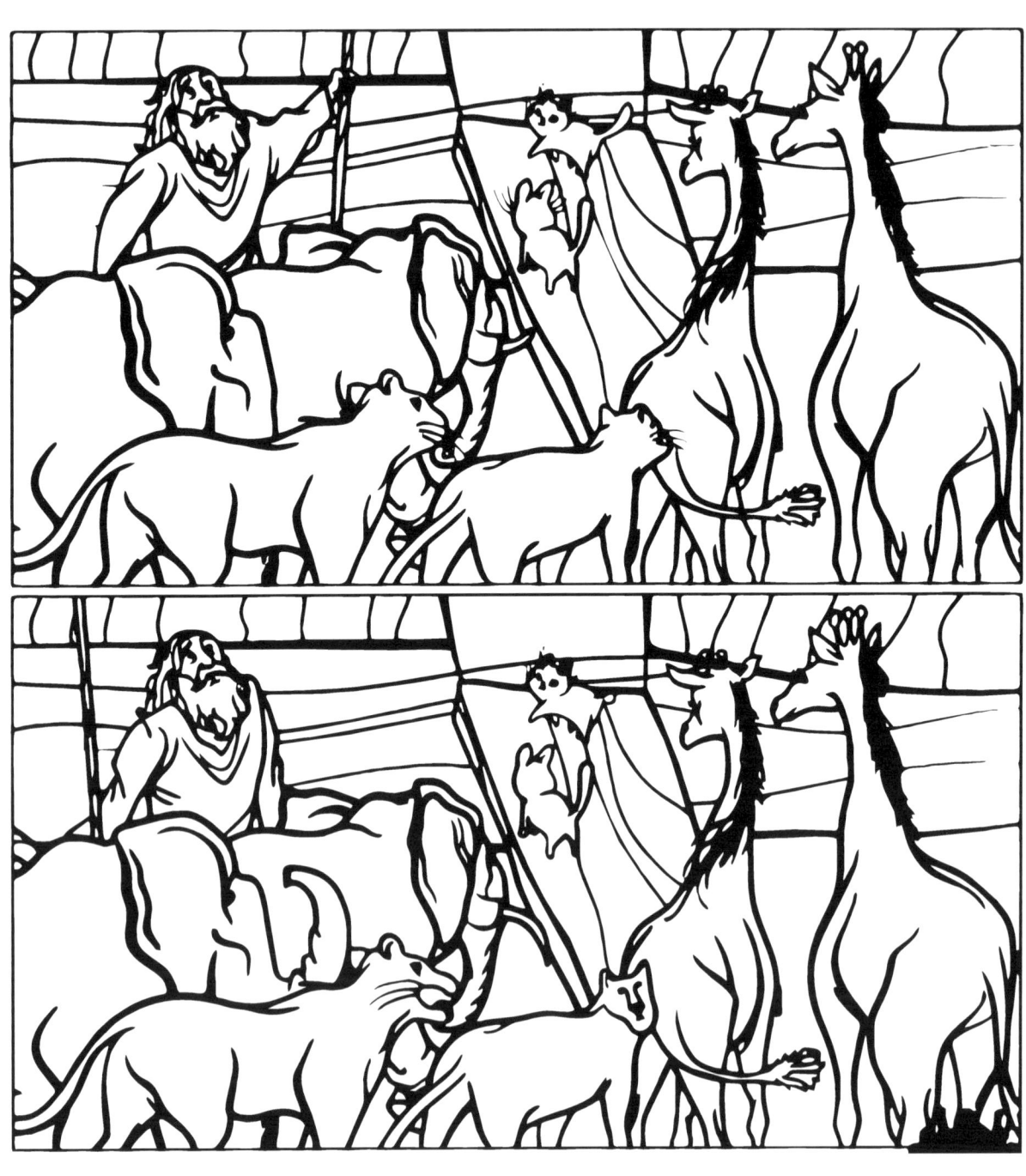

Topic: Good Communication

Introduction:

As a Christian, it's important that the virtue in us is not mingled with unrighteousness. The verse starts with "do not be deceived", let no man deceive or fool you into doing what is against the will of the Father. Jesus Himself has reiterated this in Matthew 24:11, 24. The society we are is a bad moral atmosphere that has given birth to corruption and filthiness.

Bible References:

1 Corinthians 15: 33-34
Other references:
1 Cor. 5:6, Prov. 9:6, Prov. 13:20, Psalm 1

Lessons learnt:

1. Guarding ourselves against the forces of corruption and deceit.
2. Evil communication brings destruction to the soul and the body.
3. Connecting to the source that never fails.

Assignment

How can we prevent evil communication?

Prayer

The Lord will preserve us and uphold us with His right hand of righteousness.

What I have learnt:

_____
_____
_____
_____
_____
_____

1 Corinthians 15:33
(Tune: 'This Old Man')

Do not be misled.
Bad company
corrupts good character.
1 Corinthians 15:33
Do not be misled.

Topic: The Armour of God

Introduction:

Armour is a complete pack of weapons used on the battlefield and therefore is necessary for war/combat. The essence of the armour is to defend oneself from the attack of the enemy. The passage we would be reading today explains the type of enemy we are fighting with and gave a description of such and why it's necessary for the armour to be worn always. Then verse 10 is drawing on a conclusion by using the word finally and it tells us that the power or armour is of God and should be obtained from Him

What I have learnt:

_____
_____
_____
_____
_____
_____
_____
_____
_____
_____
_____

Bible References:

Ephesians 6: 10-18

Lessons learnt:

1. Knowing and understanding a battle for everyone to fight.
2. The necessary weapon needed for the battle.
3. How we can apply the amour of God.

Activity

1. How do you view the battle from the text?
2. How can the armour be worn?

Recite Ephesians 6:1 – 'Children, obey your parents in the Lord, for this is right. "That it may go well with you and that you may enjoy long life on the earth." Fathers do not exasperate your children; instead, bring them up in the training and instruction of the Lord'.

Prayer

Dear Lord, help us to put on us Your armour.

The GCCMI Bible Club

Armor of God

Ephesians 6 11 18

Children Weekly Bible Lesson

COLOUR THIS BEAUTIFULLY

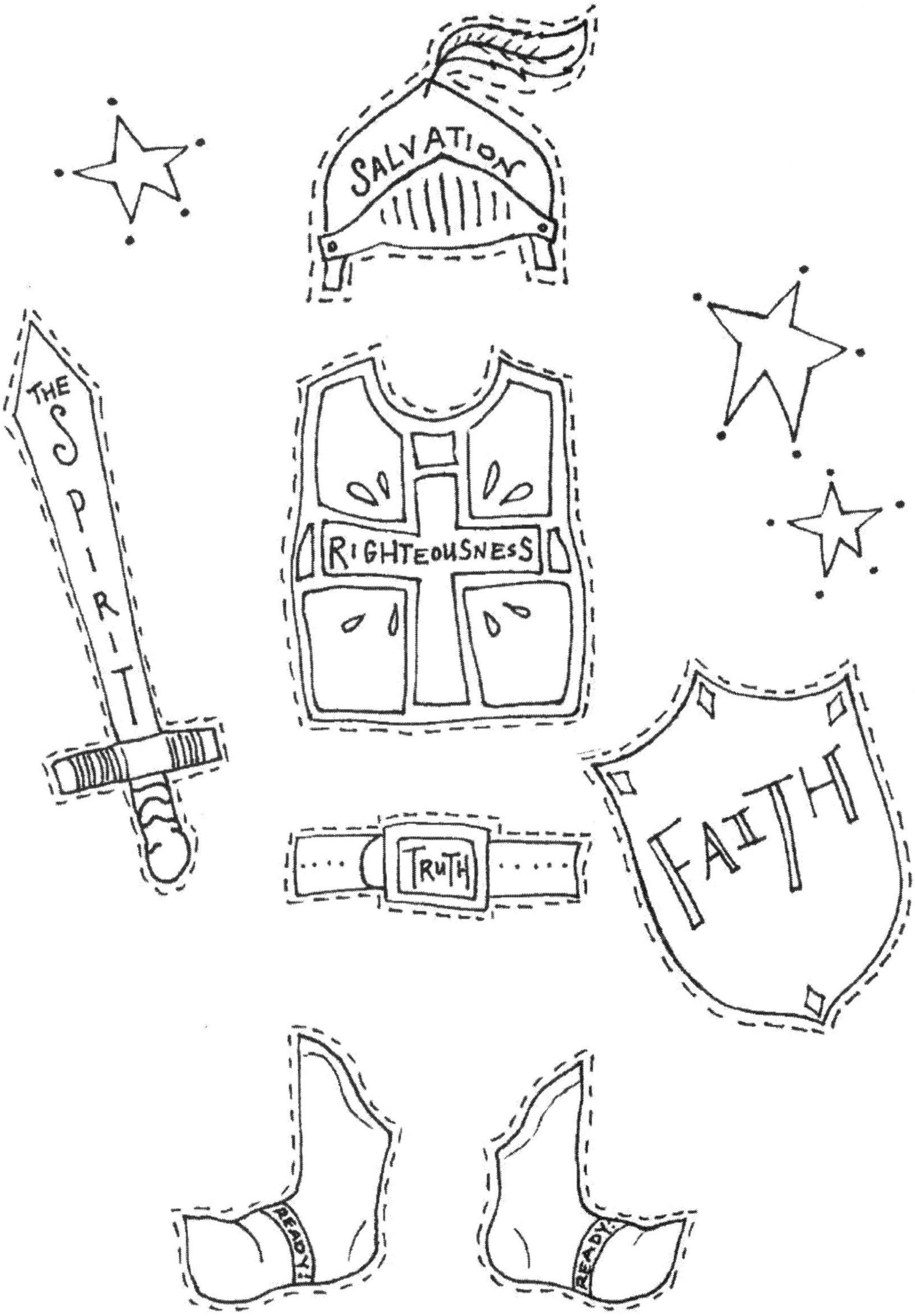

Colour the picture below.

Children Weekly Bible Lesson

Colour the picture below.

Topic: Who Is Jesus?

Introduction:

Jesus was born in Bethlehem to Hebrew parents, Mary and Joseph. At 12 years old, He was an amazing teacher with His understanding of the Old Testament. He started His teaching Ministry at about 30 years old with twelve disciples and during this time, He performed numerous miracles. Three days after His death, He rose from the grave. We have sinned, disobeyed, and become separated from God. Sometimes, we don't understand God, and by our own power, we cannot be saved or come to the Father. But Jesus lived, died, and came back to life so that we could have a way to be with Him. Jesus is one with the Father, and He is our guide to eternal life. We can believe and trust in what He says because He loves and gave Himself for us. Jesus is the Son of God. He came to earth to die for the sins of all people so that those who believed in Him could be saved. He is preparing a place for us to be in Heaven someday.

What I have learnt:

_____
_____
_____
_____
_____
_____

Bible References:

John 14: 1-14

Lessons learnt:

1. Jesus is the Son of God.
2. Jesus died for our sins.
3. Jesus is the way, the truth, and the life.

Activity:

Memory verse: John 14: 6
Discuss - Who do you think Jesus is? What does He mean to you?
Make a road map with construction paper and marker, showing given locations. Discuss how Jesus shows us the way to life.

Prayer

Thank You, Lord, for sending Jesus to die for me. Jesus, I pray that You will help me to be more conscious of You and You will reveal more of Yourself to me in Jesus' name. Amen.

Children Weekly Bible Lesson

Name:

Jesus' Birth and Childhood Activity Page

WORD SCRAMBLE/BIBLE STUDY

Look up the following verses to unscramble the words and learn facts about Jesus.

1. Matthew 2:1 - Jesus was born in_____
   HEETLEMHB

2. Matthew 1:24-25 - Jesus was the_____child in His family.
   OBFSRITRN

3. Matthew 13:55-56 - Jesus had_____and_____
   TRSBORHE   TSIRSSE

4. Matthew 1:16 - Jesus' parents were_____and_____
   PJHOSE   RMYA

5. Luke 2:39-40 - Jesus was filled_____as a child.
   MIDWOS

6. Luke 2:46 - Jesus enjoyed going to the_____
   LMEPET

7. Matthew 1:18 - Jesus' mother, Mary was a_____
   IRIVGN

8. Luke 2:25-38 - _____and_____met Jesus as a baby
   OESIMN   NAAN

Topic: What Is Giving?

Introduction:

Giving means giving out something like money, toys, or a small gift to another person. In the story we read, Jesus was observing what people were giving to the church. The rich people put in a lot of money and then a poor widow came to give all that she had. Who do you think God appreciates more? (Allow responses) Jesus explains to us that even though the rich had put in a lot of money, it was still only a little bit of what they had. But the widow gave everything she had. She gave generously. The widow wasn't worried she wouldn't have money to buy the things she needed. She trusted that God would provide. The woman worshipped God by giving with a happy heart.

God wants us to give with a cheerful heart. He doesn't want us to give because we feel that we have to. It pleases God to see that we give. We can give many things; we can give our time, money, talent, and prayers. All these help others learn about God's wonderful plan of salvation. Giving is an act of worship when we do it with the right attitude.

What I have learnt:

_____
_____
_____
_____
_____

Bible References:

Mark 12:41-44

Lessons learnt:

1. Giving is an act of worship.
2. God loves a cheerful giver.
3. Give without complaining.
4. When you give, trust God to provide for your needs.

Activity:

Have you ever had a hard time sharing something you really love? Maybe a toy or a favorite snack. How did it make you feel? Did you give cheerfully? Memorize the verse: John 3:16

Prayer

Father, thank You for Your Word. I pray that You grant me a heart that gives cheerfully, that my gifts will be pleasing to you, in Jesus' name. Amen.

Children Weekly Bible Lesson

Colour the picture nicely

What's the girl in the picture doing?

Topic: The Power of Praise

Bible References:

2 Chronicles 20:1-30

Introduction:

It can be hard, but God wants us to thank Him for everything, because hard times help us learn to trust Him more and to grow stronger in our character. If we face difficult or scary times, we can remember what Jehoshaphat did when he had a big problem. He thanked God for His love, even though the Israelites were in a discouraging and seemingly hopeless situation. And after God came to their rescue, Jehoshaphat remembered to have all of the people praise and thank God for caring for them. In today's Bible lesson, God shows His mighty power when His people turn to Him when faced with a very difficult situation.

Lessons learnt:

1. You can always trust God and believe that He has the answer to help you.
2. God fights for His children who cry out to Him and seek His help
3. God is amazing and every time He shows His power we should be in awe.
4. King Jehoshaphat's response to difficulty was to seek God's help and he pointed the people to God as well.
5. Not only did God rescue Jehoshaphat from this large army, He also gave them a large amount of treasure that took three days to collect
6. God showed His mighty power to His people by rescuing them
7. God is able to do more than we can imagine and is worthy of all worship.

Activity:

Sing a song that praises God.

Prayer

Dear God, please help me to be joyful and full of your praise always and to remember to give You thanks for all things

Assignment:

1. Write about a time when God helped when you or someone who was in a difficult situation.
   ....
   ....

2. What difficulty was Jehoshaphat facing?
   ....
   ....

3. How did Jehoshaphat respond when he heard the alarming news?
   ....

4. How were the soldiers to fight this battle?
   ....

5. Who went before the soldiers as they went to the battlefield?
   ....

6. How did God rescue Jehoshaphat from his enemies?
   ....

7. How much treasure did Jehoshaphat and his soldiers find?
   ....

8. What was Jehoshaphat and the soldiers' response to God's help?
   ....

What I have learnt:

_____

_____

_____

_____

_____

_____

_____

_____

_____

GIVE THANKS TO THE LORD

Spot 8 differences between the two pictures.

Topic: God will never change

Introduction:

Can someone answer me this, name ways that you have changed this year? Can you also name various things that have changed around you? We can change very easily and in fact people and all other parts of creation are always changing, but God never changes. What were you like as a baby, what are you like now and what do you think you'll be like when you are a grown up?

Lessons learnt:

1. God is unchangeable = cannot be moved, does not change.
2. We change as we grow but God NEVER changes
3. The whole Bible is the story of God coming into His creation and changing people's hearts (Ezekiel 36:26)
4. The fact that we can't change our sinful hearts on our own reminds us of the unchanging nature of God. Only God can change our hearts

What I have learnt:

Bible References:

Heb 1:11-12

Activity:

Write the word UNCHANGEABLE and frame it

Prayer

Lord, I pray I come to know You more and more each week through this study and as I think of the many different ways that I have changed. I am rejoicing in the fact that I have a God that never changes.

Assignment:

Answer this riddle; there's someone you know, He is loving, caring, holy, great, powerful, knowledgeable, kind, beautiful, merciful and He never changes, who is He?

....

God Never Changes Picture Game

(Ages 7-10)

Below are pictures of things that change. Can you name how they change and what they become? Aren't you glad that God never changes! "Jesus Christ is the same yesterday, today, and forever." (Hebrews 13:8).

#1. baby girl

#2. caterpillar

#3. tadpole

#4. puppy

#5. seeds

#6. water

#7. rain

#8. chick

Topic: The Parable - God's Kingdom is a Treasure

Bible References:
Matthew 13:44-50

Introduction:

Who can remind us what parables are? Today's story is one of Jesus' parables. Can you think of anything so wonderful in this life that you would sell EVERYTHING you have to get it? A new car, a new phone or a swimming pool in your backyard. But would you be willing to sell ALL your clothes, ALL your toys, your cars, your food, and even your house to get any of those things? No way! Nothing in this life is worth selling ALL your stuff in exchange for. But the Kingdom of Heaven is worth everything we have and then some. As citizens of the Kingdom of Heaven, we are willing to give up everything to follow Jesus, and we tell everyone about how much Jesus loves them.

Lessons learnt:

1. The man stumbled on the field he wasn't looking for the treasure (it reminds us that Jesus is calling everyone to himself, even those who aren't looking for him.)
2. Jesus loves everyone and wants everyone to follow him, even the people that don't seem to want to have anything to do with him.
3. The treasure in this parable is the Kingdom of Heaven
4. Heaven is where we get to spend all of forever with Jesus, our King. It is the best treasure we could ever want!

Activity:

Song – My God is so big
My God is so big! So strong and so mighty.
There's nothing my God cannot do (clap-clap).
The mountains are his and the valleys are his
and the trees are his handiwork too.
https://youtu.be/DYwxCCrGkUU

Prayer

Dear Lord, we thank you for promising that we will get to go to Heaven someday. Amen.

Assignment:

1. In the parable, what did the man find hidden in a field?
   ....

2. In the parable, why did the merchant sell everything he had?
   ....
   ....
   ....
   ....

3. What is the lesson of the Parable of the Hidden Treasure?
   ....
   ....
   ....
   ....
   ....

What I have learnt:

Connect the dots and then colour the picture.

"The kingdom of heaven is like treasure hidden in a field. When a man found it, he hid it again, and then in his joy went and sold all he had and bought that field." Matthew 13:44

Treasure in the Field Maze

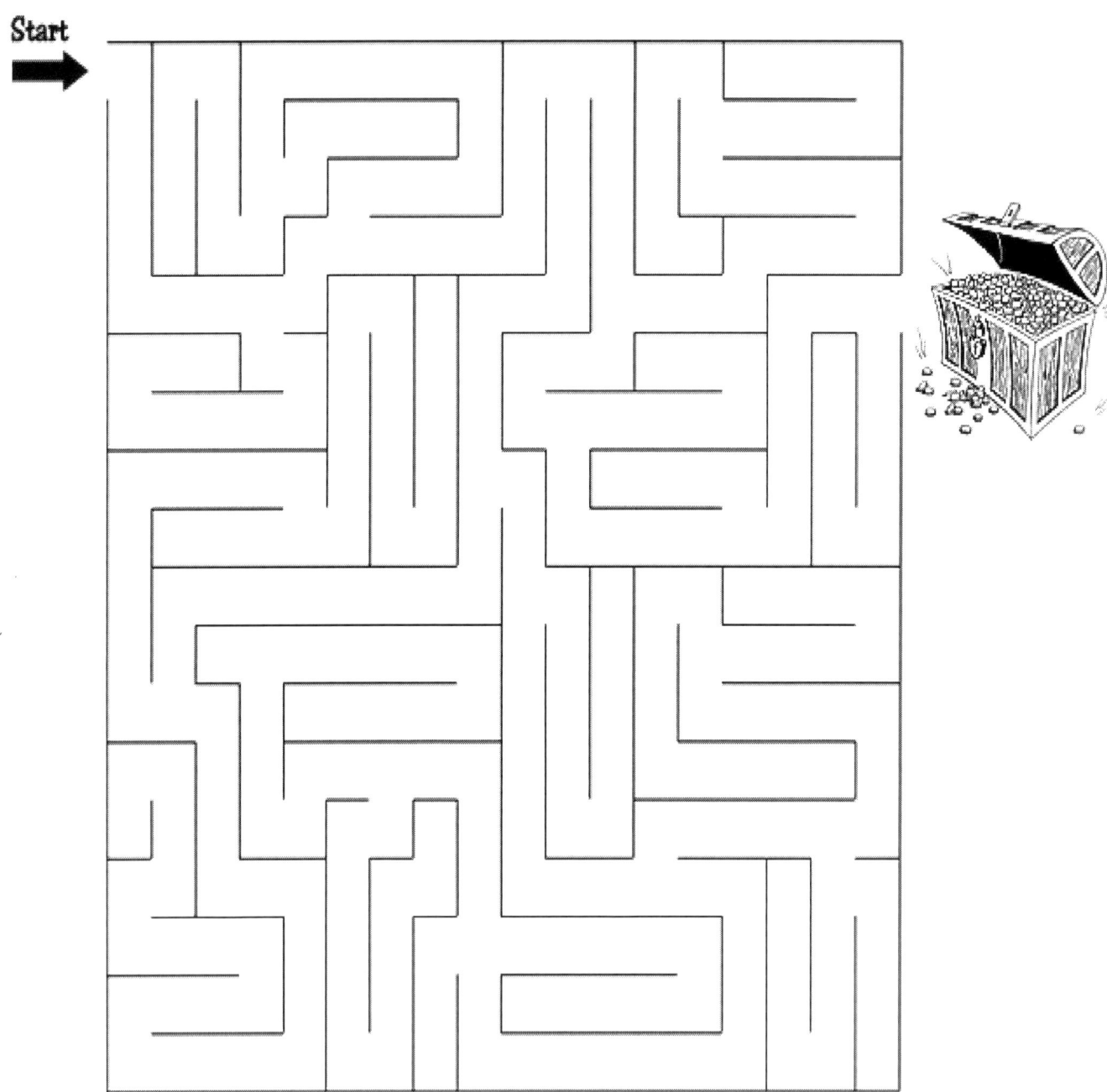

Can you find the way to the hidden treasure?

Topic: The Parable of the Unforgiving Servant

Bible References: Matthew 18:21-35

Introduction:

How many times can you do various tasks? How many pushups can you do? How many times can you bounce a basketball? How many times can you kick a ball in the air? Can we do any of these activities 490 times? Today, we will learn one way that we are supposed to behave as Christians. Follow along with me as I read from Matthew 18:21-35.

Lessons learnt:

1. As citizens of the Kingdom of Heaven, we forgive others their debt against us since Jesus forgave our debt against him.
2. The Bible tells us in 1 Corinthians 13:5 that love keeps no record of wrongs.
3. Jesus does not want us to literally forgive 490 times, He gives this really big number for two reasons. One is to tell us that we should forgive endlessly.
4. The other reason he gives us such a big number is to tell us that we cannot forgive endlessly on our own. We need Jesus to help us forgive.

What I have learnt:

_____
_____
_____
_____
_____

Activity:

Is it easy to forgive people who wronged us?
Think of something wrong someone said or did to you recently. Remember that God wants you to forgive others. Pray silently to God for a few seconds and ask God to help you forgive them.

Prayer

Lord, please grant us the desire to want to learn how to forgive as you do. When we beg for forgiveness, you readily grant it. All is wiped clean, all is forgotten.

Assignment:

Share-a-Heart. Cut out a heart shape from a piece of paper (Have an adult help you), decorate it and write on it "God loves us and forgives us." Think of someone with whom you would like to share your paper heart.

Children Weekly Bible Lesson

Forgiving Your Brother Word Search

```
X N Z J D T E T P D R S R R O
W V N E D V S A X E W R X B F
O X K L I N C U O V T K U E M
K S I G I X S F P Y X E Y I G
A U R A F A W I M A N Y R G E
K O G J E O D O N Q H Q Z P Z
F A F S J V F I U S V U H G B
R E E L E S J E S U S W V P P
B R O T H E R E F W W I E X E
L B D G E V E T N Z Z W W E C
V I L Y T E V D D S E Z E E Z
G P M Y I N A R J F V O R T X
B B J I M R O A E X Z Y Z Y Q
C A M E E L B X R C U K J A L
L K M W S H V O Q Z B M K L T
```

Peter	Jesus	times	sins
came	Lord	forgive	against
asked	many	brother	seven

The GCCMI Bible Club

Topic: The Parable - Lost Things Get Found

Bible References: Luke 15:1-32

Introduction:

What is a Parable? Today, we are going to look at three stories today from Luke 15:1-32. All of these stories have the same main point. What does that tell you? If Jesus told three different stories to get this point across, that tells us that this is a very important message. So, follow along closely as I read from Luke 15:1-32. In each story, someone loses something precious to them. When they find it, they celebrate. God rejoices when lost sinners come to him, and we should too. As citizens of the Kingdom of Heaven, we help people get to know God, and we celebrate when they give their lives to him.

Lessons learnt:

1. God rejoices when lost sinners come to Him and we should too
2. We are to search for lost sinners and tell them about Jesus as citizens of the Kingdom of Heaven
3. God is loving and forgiving

Activity:

I'm all wrapped up, all tied up, all tangled up in Jesus.
I'm all wrapped up, all tied up, all tangled up in God.
I'm all wrapped up, all tied up, all tangled up in Jesus.
I'm all wrapped up, all tied up, all tangled up in God.
https://youtu.be/RWp1IsEK7yQ

What I have learnt:

_____
_____
_____
_____
_____
_____
_____
_____
_____

Prayer

Dear God, thank you for your grace, thank you for forgiving our sins We know we do bad things, but you still call us your kids! Thank you for your love, Lord, we love you! Thanks for sending Jesus, In His name we pray, Amen

Children Weekly Bible Lesson

BIBLE QUIZ

THE PRODIGAL SON

Match the question with the answer on the right.

Questions

____ How many sons did the father have?

____ Which son asked his father for his inheritance?

____ After he left home, where did the son go?

____ What happened in the country where the son went?

____ After the son wasted his money, what job did he get?

____ Why did the son decide to return home?

____ Who was not happy about the son's return?

____ What did the father do when he saw his youngest son in the distance?

____ What did the father give his son when he arrived home?

____ What did the father do to celebrate his youngest son's return?

Answers

1. There was a famine
2. Feeding pigs
3. Good shoes, clothes and a ring.
4. The eldest son
5. Youngest son
6. Two
7. Far away country
8. Ran to his son, threw his arms around him and kissed him.
9. He came to his senses (repentance).
10. Killed a fatted calf and had a party.

Unscramble the letters to find the words in our

Prodigal Son Anagram

Word List:
celebrate, family, father, forgiveness, found, home, hungry, inheritance, pigs, prodigal

adgilopr _____

aefhrt _____

aceehiinnrt _____

afilmy _____

ghnruy _____

gips _____

ehmo _____

abceeelrt _____

eefginorssv _____

dfnou _____

GCC Ministry International

For more information, please contact:
574 Gorgie Road Edinburgh Scotland EH11 3AL, United Kingdom
Phone: **00447563803455**
Email address: **info@gloriouschristianchildren.com**
Follow us on YouTube: **GCCM International**
Website: **www.gccmi.co.uk**

Printed in Great Britain
by Amazon